This book is dedicated to

AUSTIN & BETTY PAUL

of the Africa Inland Mission

with genuine admiration, appreciation, and affection.

Evangelist Bill Rice, Author

CONTENTS

FOREWORD

The Austin Pauls were my hosts during the months of revival campaigns in Africa. They made an everlasting impression upon me for God and for good.

Bwana Paul was lean and wiry, fast on his feet, and fast of mind. He was quick-witted in every situation. A veteran missionary with thirty years of experience, he had a ready answer for everything, whether it was how to get the Pie-wagon across a river, how to start a fire in the rain, or how to advise a heartbroken native about any given subject.

He also had a hair-trigger temper! Oddly enough, however, I never knew him to be really angry with any particular person over anything. And I never knew him to be angry over anything of more importance than the time he couldn't find the right screwdriver to fix the amplifier. He stood beside the old Pie-wagon and denounced the villain who had taken his screwdriver out of the tool box and forgotten to replace it. If he had to, he stormed, he was going to put a dozen locks on that thing so no one could bother his tools without his permission.

It is my firm conviction that he would still be standing there yelling about that screwdriver if Mrs. Paul had not gently asked him what that bulgy thing in his jacket pocket was!

But in any kind of an emergency he was not only calm and clear-headed but disgustingly cheerful. If we had a flat tire on the wagon at three o'clock in the morning when all of us were so tired we could hardly breathe, he would open the door and swing out of the car as cheerfully as a boy getting up on Christmas morning. There were times when we lost our food, there were times when we drove at night and lost our way, there were times when we were desperately sick with malaria or with dysentery; but I never knew him to lose either his cheerfulness, his optimism, or his soul-winning fervor.

We worked together for several months, day and night, often under the most trying of circumstances, and he never said one word to me, at any time, that was not courteous and gracious and friendly.

I loved him then and I love him now—deeply, sincerely, and gratefully.

Mrs. Paul, on the other hand, was of a quiet and meek disposition. She was (she has since gone to Heaven) surely one of the finest ladies it has ever been my good fortune to know. She endured hardship that many women do not dream even exists and she endured it graciously, as unto the Lord. She was exactly the kind of wife Austin Paul needed.

Surely the Lord was never more wise than when He brought these two together as man and wife!

Like the New Testament Paul

The Apostle Paul of the New Testament and the Austin Paul of the Congo had much in common. I think I have never known a more fervent, up-and-at-'em soul winner than Austin Paul. Literally everywhere we went—and we traveled hundreds of miles—I met his converts. Again and again, we would be driving down a dusty trail and stop at a small village because *Bwana* Paul would tell me he had some "children" there. We would walk into the village, and sure enough, there would be his converts, absolutely delighted at seeing him again. I have seen men and women weep as he told them good-by to continue his journey.

Going into a large village one day, the chief came and fell at Austin Paul's feet, saying over and over, through his tears, "My spiritual father! You have come back to see us and to bless us again!"

Godly Missionaries

I was the key speaker at the bi-annual missionary fellowship at Rethy and so I met most of the A.I.M. missionaries not on furlough. I met many of them again as we traveled in revivals from station to station. And I met many missionaries connected with organizations other than the A.I.M. Since our revivals usually lasted only one week, I did not get as well acquainted with many of these wonderful people as I would have liked. All in all, I found them to be men and women of stalwart Christian character and many of them were fervent soul winners.

I immediately liked Jim and Agnes Bell, who had a mud house with thatched roof at Oicha (O-wee-chee), but who spent much of their time at Biasiku where they lived and worked with Pygmies.

Harold and Jane Amstutz made a lasting impression upon me. He is a large, handsome man and she is a very beautiful woman. Both sing well and she is an excellent pianist. Friends thought they were wasting their lives by taking such talent to the Dark Continent. But, with their son, David, they did a magnificent work for Christ. They also suffered fiery trials that would have crushed lesser Christians.

Multiplied thousands of people have heard me tell of them on revival platforms throughout the nation.

Another couple I loved and admired was the Sid Langfords at Aba. They were of that heroic stuff from which pioneers are made. They also had the kind of faith that produces lasting results.

It was a privilege to know Dr. and Mrs. Carl Becker at Oicha. Here was the second largest leper colony in all the world plus the largest and busiest jungle hospital in the world. I took moving pictures of Dr. Becker in his operating room. "Don't take a picture of my face," he said. "When people see these pictures let them simply think of me as the representative of all the missionaries." He probably operates on as many patients in one term as most physicians do in a lifetime of practice. Until I saw him in action, I had never realized the importance of medical missionaries.

Then there were so many, many others—the Paul Stoughs, the Claudon Stauffachers, Dr. and Mrs. Ralph Kleinschmidt, Misses Mary Heyward, Olive Rawn and Jewell Olson, Bill Deans (the Plymouth Brethren missionary), the Paul Hurlburts, Mr. and Mrs. Gurney Harris, Mr. and Mrs. Andy Uhlinger, Mr. and Mrs. George Van Duesen, Mr. and Mrs. George Stuart, and the William Beattys.

We did all of our traveling in a Metro delivery truck, the kind so many companies use for the delivery of bread, cakes, etc. We called it the "Pie-wagon." However, on the inside we had bus seats instead of shelves, and windows were installed in the sides of the truck.

In the Pie-wagon traveled our revival team, including the Pauls and me and four natives who worked full-time with Austin. He had taught them to read music and play brass instruments—three trumpets and one valve trombone. Big Solomono was oldest, happy

Methuselah was youngest, Ephrenoto often preached, and Juano was the quiet one. We lived with these black men for months and I learned to love each one.

A "Zip-by" Missionary

Referring to a fellow who wrote about life in the West, an old-timer called him a "zip-by" cowboy, explaining that all he knew about the West was what he had seen as he "zipped by" on a train. So I am, I fear, a "zip-by" missionary.

And I realize that an amateur does not see things through the eyes of an expert. Some years ago, four men from Pennsylvania came to visit me on the Ranch. One day I took them riding—a new experience for each of them. We were back in the Big Pasture when we suddenly came upon six or eight horses I had previously spent several days searching for. I yelled to my companions that I was going to try to get these horses to the corral and that they would find their way back by following the pioneer road. With that, I dashed into the brush, headed the horses toward the corral, and chased them home. A few minutes later, my four friends, hanging onto their saddles for dear life, came galloping back. Their horses, left to themselves, had simply returned to the stable.

I thought nothing of the experience until the following year when I went to their church for a revival campaign. Everyone there knew about the day we had driven up the "wild" horses and of the perilous ride that they had made, leaping over brush and ditches on the way back to the corrals! A commonplace occurrence to me had been an unusual adventure for them.

So, admittedly, I am an amateur as far as missionary work in Africa is concerned. Just the same, they were days of soul winning and revival and exciting adventure. We were in some situations that even veteran missionaries had never experienced before! And we saw some things that even Austin Paul, in his thirty years, had never seen.

I believe you will find these stories refreshing and different than anything you have ever read before. To the thousands of young people who will be reading this book, may I remind you that there is still a need today for dedicated young men and women to serve Christ in the continent of Africa.

(I have just learned that Austin Paul and his beloved Betty are together again. While still serving Christ in Nyunkunde, Congo, *Bwana* Paul was transferred to Heaven on February 3, 1968.)

1

BIBLES, BOOTS, CAMERAS, AND GUNS!

It was at famous Moody Memorial Church in Chicago that I met Austin Paul. I was one of the speakers of the Founder's Week Conference. It was the evening of Wednesday, February 4, 1948, and I had just preached on soul winning, using as my text,

"He that goeth forth and weepeth, bearing precious seed, shall doubtless come again with rejoicing, bringing his sheaves with him."—Psalm 126:6.

After the services were over that night, a slender, energetic man with a touch of gray in his temple, clear sharp eyes, and an alertness it is hard to describe, walked up to me.

"My name is Austin Paul," he said, "I am a missionary with the Africa Inland Mission. You are a man after my own heart! How about coming to the Congo for some revival campaigns?"

"When?" I asked as we shook hands.

"In about two years," he replied. "It will take me that long to get set up for really large revivals." "All right," I said, "I'll come!"

It was as simple as that. In approximately ten seconds and with a man I had never even heard before, I had arranged to fly all the way to Africa to spend three months in revival campaigns.

In talking about it later that night, the Princess and I both agreed that it was of the Lord. But it did seem strange to her, she said, that I had so readily accepted an invitation from a total stranger when it was going to cost us so much money and time.

"Austin Paul is no stranger," I told her. "After you know him one second, you have known him all your life."

Raising the Money

It was more than a year later when I said to my lovely wife, "Princess, I don't know how in the world I am going to get the money to go to Africa. It is going to take hundreds of dollars and I don't know where it is going to come from."

At first I had thought I would write to a number of pastors with whom I had conducted revival campaigns, asking them to take up an expense offering for me. But the more I thought of it, the less I liked the idea. I had never one time written back to any church where I had conducted a revival campaign and asked for additional money. I had never even written back to a church hinting for money. I had never written back asking any church to pray for my financial needs. And I simply did not feel it would please the Lord for me to do so now.

But what was I going to do? I not only needed money for my plane fare and other traveling expenses but for Cathy and the four children to live on while I was gone.

But if I did not know where to get the money, my lovely wife did. "We can sell our house," she said. "It should sell for five times as much as we will need."

Sell our home in Wheaton! The house we had lived in for eight years! The house we had paid for once, then borrowed some money for mission work and almost had paid out again! The house with the great big living room where I practiced calf roping on Super, our Great Dane dog!

After the initial shock was over, we sat down and talked about it, and I agreed that this was what we should do. The Princess, it turned out, had thought all the time that this would be the solution to our financial problem. "I know you would never write anybody and ask for money," she grinned.

So we put our house up for sale. And since we were going to sell it so I could go to Africa, we decided we would put all of the money into missionary work.

We had decided that after I had spent three months in Africa, Cathy would meet me in Cairo and we would go on to Palestine. After all, my plane ticket would cost very little extra, so it would be an opportunity for both of us to visit Palestine for the price of one. We decided to borrow the money from the bank to pay for her plane fare and the money it would take for us to live on while touring the Holy Land. But when we dropped by to see the president of the bank to ask for a loan, he reminded us that we already had more than enough money to take the trip.

"Why do you want to borrow money when you already have more than six thousand dollars in your account?" he asked. "Because," I answered, "we have decided not to use that money—it really isn't ours and we are trying to decide what to do with it."

Our friend's mouth popped open and he stared at us in amazement. "Oh, oh, oh, Mr. Rice," he said in a shocked voice.

It turned out he thought I meant we had stolen the money! Cathy and I burst out laughing and then explained to him that we had dedicated that money to God and could not use it for our personal needs. He looked at us incredulously as we explained and then made out a check for the money we needed.

Weights and Measures

Austin Paul wrote and suggested I bring a high-powered game rifle with me. But I decided against it. I love hunting too much and did not want it to sidetrack me from the revival ministry for which I was going to Africa. I did decide, however, to take with me a fine .357 Magnum revolver that a sheriff in Waterloo, Iowa, had secured for me.

(Actually, it turned out that Austin Paul had known what he was talking about because I did do a great deal of hunting. It was either hunt or do without meat.)

The Magnum six-shooter had just been developed and it was a dandy. It would handle ordinary .38 caliber cartridges or the .357 Magnum bullets. With the Magnum cartridges, it was the most powerful handgun in the world. It would actually fire a steel bullet through a V-8 Ford engine!

I bought forty boxes of ammunition to take with me.

I also felt it important that I take a motion picture camera and a still camera with me. Mr. Baptista purchased an excellent Bolex for me at wholesale cost and a professor in Indiana did the same with an Eastman 35mm slide camera. The Life brothers In Clarksburg, West Virginia, made me a present of an expensive telephoto and wide-angle lens and gave me several hundred dollars' worth of color film.

Of course, I was going to take along a pair of boots. After all, what would any well-dressed man in Africa wear if not cowboy boots!

I also wanted to take my Scofield Bible, a larger Kirkbride Reference Bible, and John Rice's book, "PRAYER Asking and Receiving."

When I packed my suitcase, I was delighted that it was a perfect fit—a gun here, a camera there, boots in that corner, ammunition here…what's more, when I closed the suitcase and weighed it on the scales—it weighed just exactly what I was allowed to carry! Talk about luck!

But the Princess burst out laughing and shaking her head sadly at the same time. When she could speak she said, "Of course you have packed the *essentials*— but since you will be gone six months don't you think you ought to take along some clothes to wear?"

Great guns! I had been so interested in packing Bibles and cameras and guns and stuff that I had not packed a single shirt, sock, or suit! Not even a change of underwear!

I called the airport and found out that every pound over weight would cost me a fortune. I was told, however, that I might carry as much as I liked in my pockets. So the Princess and I taped packages of film together and stuffed them in my trouser pockets, coat pockets, and topcoat pockets. Most of the ammunition I left behind, and more than half of the film I shipped to Africa. (It arrived three months later, just two days before I left Africa to go to Palestine.)

So, there came a January day that I boarded a plane in Nashville that would take me to New York City, Europe, and Africa. I'll bet the crew on that airplane still talks about the tall passenger in cowboy boots with his arms full of cameras and his pockets bulging for all the world like a pickpocket from Possum Trot!

My First Letter Home

"Precious Princess—

"*Africa at last! I stood before the grass hut that serves as an administration office and waiting room for the little grass field honored by the name 'airport' and looked around. Almost naked natives were already swarming over the huge four-engined Babena airliner, putting in gas and oil, hooking on starter batteries, etc. At the door of the grass hut stood a pot-bellied native soldier dressed in khaki shorts, a red fez, and a wide leather belt. He had wrap-around leggings on his skinny legs and his black feet were bare. One of the tallest men I ever saw in my life was walking down the dusty trail. He was as black as night and as naked as the day he was born! 'Yep, this is Africa all right, 'I thought as I followed a man to the station wagon that was to take me on to the Belgian Congo.*

"*One hundred fifty miles of smoke-like dust, yelling natives, then to the mission station that was to be headquarters for the next several months.*

"*Austin Paul meets me in the Pie-wagon. He is grinning, his hair is graying, his eyes a keen brown, his voice jovial, his body slim, his movements quick and vigorous. He is to be my companion, manager, guide, interpreter, and host during my stay. Around us are tropical fruit trees—bananas, oranges, and papaya. In the sky, a torrid tropical sun. On the ground beside me is a suitcase of clothes, two leather-cased cameras, film, and tripod. I am dressed in a sport shirt and slacks. On my head is a Stetson hat. Around my middle is a heavy gun belt and holster containing a powerful .38 six-shooter and 100 rounds of ammunition. On my feet are soft, low-cut flying boots. In my pocket is a billfold with pictures of my wife, my children, my song leader, dog, pet lion, and about seventy dollars. In my hand, a Scofield Bible, a Kirkbride Bible, and John Rice's book, 'PRAYER Asking and Receiving'....*

"*Okay—I'm here for revivals—let's get going!*"

2

HOME SWEET HOME

Eight Goats for a Bride

When I was there, the going price for an African bride was eight goats. Of course, if she were an unusually beautiful or strong or healthy girl, she might be worth nine or even ten goats, with a clay pot or a handful of fried ants thrown in to complete the bargain.

One of Austin Paul's converts was a blind man. This fellow took the name of Paula. Being blind and very poor, he could not afford a wife. Finally they heard of a man who had a marriageable daughter for sale. But the girl was so ugly that the father had been unable to find a buyer. Naturally, therefore, he reduced the price. Even at a bargain price, however, there were no takers.

Finally, the price was so low that blind Paula managed to scrape up enough money to purchase the goats he could exchange for the girl. But when blind Paula came with the "treasure," the old man upped the price. After all, he argued, Paula was blind. What if the girl were ugly—Paula would never know the difference!

The controversy was brought to the chief, who decided in favor of Paula. It was not fair, he said, to penalize a man because he was unfortunate enough to be blind. After all, he probably needed a wife more than most men. Furthermore, the girl needed a husband and it was obvious that a man who could see her wasn't going to buy her!

So, blind Paula got his bride and the girl was won to Christ. When I saw them, they both appeared to be happy Christians.

Who Walks in Front

The wife is completely the possession of her husband. The ordinary native is likely to regard his wife in much the same way he regards his goat. She is important to him in proportion to what she can do for him.

His regard for her is shown in many ways, particularly in the matter of dress. The natives, on a whole, admire the white man and they like to wear his clothes. I have actually seen a native man wearing a heavy army overcoat on a steaming hot day! The sweat pouring off his face, he proudly struts around in his coat. I have seen them wearing nothing but ragged shorts (standard dress for men) and a necktie! I also saw a man wearing leather leggings and a loincloth!

Frequently, men will wear two or three pair of trousers at the same time. One day we met a man and his wife. He was wearing three pair of trousers and she was naked except for an apron of green leaves. Austin Paul asked him why he did not trade one pair of trousers for some cloth so that his wife might have something to wear. The man looked at *Bwana* Paul in amazement. "*Bwana*," he said, "if you had more than one pair of trousers would you put one pair of them on your goat?" If a man would not dress up his goat, why should he dress up his wife!

Men hunt and that is about all the work they do. The wives take care of the garden, do the cooking (men are served first and women may eat what is left over), and take care of the children.

Time and again I have seen a man walking down a trail carrying nothing but himself. Behind him will come his wives carrying children and other burdens on their backs and on their heads. The man walks in front and the women walk in single file behind—that's the way it should be! But should a man be walking behind one of his wives, that means that family unity has been disrupted. She has done something that has displeased her husband and is probably going to get a licking for it just as soon as he gets her home!

The Lord and Master Gets Clobbered

Although the wife is the possession of her husband, she isn't as helpless as one might think. One day after a service, *Bwana* Paul and I drove to a small village where there was someone he wanted to visit. We had just finished a service and I was hot and tired and soaking wet with perspiration. So *Bwana* suggested that I sit in the Pie-wagon and wait for him to come back.

I was leaning back in my seat, half asleep, when I was startled with the sound of a fight and the screams of a woman. I sat up and there, right in front of the Pie-wagon, a native man was beating his wife. As they struggled, he hit her with his fist, slapped her with his hands, and kicked her with his feet. I looked around for *Bwana* Paul, but he was nowhere to be seen. Oddly enough, in spite of the ruckus, no one came running up to see what all the noise was about. I wondered what in the world I should do. Should I jump out and try to separate them? If I did and he fought, should I fight?

While I was considering what to do, the man suddenly threw the woman to the ground, kicked her several times, and then turned and began walking away. But he didn't get very far. The wife, jumping to her feet, picked up a broken limb and, running up behind him, hit him across the head!

He fell as if he had been hit with a sledge hammer. She looked at him for a moment, threw down the club, and then quickly ran out of sight. I jumped out of the Pie-wagon and ran over to him as he began to sit up, rubbing his head and looking about in a dazed fashion. About that time *Bwana* Paul returned and we helped the man to his feet.

As we drove away the man was slowly walking, still rubbing his head, in the direction his wife had taken.

I remarked that he would probably beat her half to death when he caught her, but *Bwana* Paul didn't think so. She had probably gone back to her father's house, he said, and the husband would probably have to pay another goat to the father to get the girl back again! Since no man can afford to spend his goats too freely, it was likely that he would be real nice to her for some time to come.

A Good Investment

Polygamy is a way of life to people in many parts of the world, although it seems so strange to us. Actually, it makes good sense to the unsaved natives.

In the first place, buying a wife is an investment. Because of the artificial emphasis placed on sex in America, we usually find it impossible to think of polygamy as anything other than pure, unadulterated lust. The fact is, however, that sex is only one of the reasons a man wants as many wives as possible. She is a good financial investment.

If he has several wives, then he has several who will take care of his garden and will prepare his meals. As he grows older he faces the problem that the wives of his youth have grown older also. So, it is important that he have some younger wives to take care of his older wives and to take care of him.

Then, too, the more wives, the more children; and children mean prosperity. He can sell the girls for "wealth," and the boys will probably grow up to marry and live in the same village with their father. If the family becomes large enough, they will move off to themselves and begin a new village. But this cannot be done unless the family is a large one. There is safety in numbers—safety from the attack of bands of marauders, safety from wild animals, and even safety from a shortage of baby-sitters or men to go on a hunt or nurses in time of sickness.

When the men are saved, they usually face the problem of what to do with their extra wives. It is wonderful, that having been born again, they usually are willing to be the husband of only one wife, according to the teaching of the Bible. But it is a very serious problem as to what to do with the other wives. Being a Christian, he cannot sell them to other men, nor can he simply send them away to shift for themselves.

Sometimes he will choose one wife—often his first wife—and live with her. The others he will keep in separate huts as members of the family but no longer live with them as husband and wife.

Don't Brag on the Baby

One day in a native village, we walked past a young mother nursing her baby. Using about half of my total *Bangala* vocabulary, I said, "Good pretty baby."

I thought, of course, that the mother would be pleased. I expected her to smile and nod pleasantly.

Instead, however, she yanked the nursing baby away from her breast, slammed him belly-down across the lap, and slapped him *hard* on his bare bottom. The baby, of course, began to scream;

and the young mother picked him up and shook him while yelling something at me.

I was so surprised I just stood there, wondering what I ought to say or do. Austin Paul, however, said something to the young mother and then motioned me to come alone with him. As we walked, he explained to me that the unsaved natives fear *Satani*, the Devil. They know that Satan hates them and that he is cruel and heartless. So, if Satan knew the mother thought her baby was precious to her, the Devil might disfigure the baby, make it sick, or even kill it! For this reason, it was extremely bad taste to ever compliment the parents on their little one!

It was for this reason that parents often tried to fool *Satani* by calling their babies such disparaging names as "Utterly Worthless," "Much Trouble," and "Ugly Monkey." I even heard of one baby that was named "Even a Dog Would Laugh."

"Who Killed My Wife?"

We usually had five services a day during a revival campaign. Sometimes we would have four services between sunup and noon and then a big service at night. Sometimes we would have two services in the morning, two in the afternoon, and one at night. In afternoons that we did not have revival services, we would often have a market meeting or a service in some village.

One afternoon we drove to the foot of a small mountain, got out of the Pie-wagon and walked for a couple of miles, following a winding trail that led to the village on the top of the mountain.

The grass huts of the village formed one large circle, with a council hut in the very center. The people were absolutely delighted to have us come. They were thrilled when Austin Paul's quartet joined him in playing on the trumpets. Then I brought the message.

We were hot and tired and sat down to rest in the shade for awhile before making the walk back down the mountain. A number of natives had professed Christ and some of them now brought us gifts. One woman brought me a live chicken and three eggs. Another brought *Bwana* Paul a small stalk of bananas. So we sat in the shade, drinking water from our canteens and munching on the delicious bananas.

As we sat there, the entire village began walking and running around and around our shelter and singing, "This has been a great occasion. This has been a wonderful affair. This has been a time we will remember."

I said the entire village joined in this triumphant procession. I should have said the entire village except for one man. In a hut near the spring he sat in his darkened doorway.

This man had a problem to solve. He had to find out who had been responsible for the death of his wife. She had died just a few days earlier and he had not yet found out the one responsible for her death. But he was sure of one thing—someone had put a curse on his wife. Otherwise, why should she die?

It is hard for us to understand but, as far as the ordinary African native is concerned, no one ever dies through accident or natural causes. Any time a person dies, unless he is very, very old, he has died because of a curse.

So this bereaved and embittered man was searching the faces of those who marched past his hut. Which one of them, he wondered, was responsible for the death of his wife? He would find out, he promised himself, and when he did…he fingered the razor-sharp edge of his machete.

When it was finally time for us to depart, almost everyone in the village walked part of the way down the mountain with us. When we came to the place on the trail where they would turn back, we paused for prayer and sincerely thanked God for the wonderful occasion.

It was the next day that the brooding husband discovered the "murderer" of his wife. Of course the entire village knew what was on his mind, and many of them also wondered who the guilty person might be. On the day following our meeting, he seated himself by the spring where the women came for water. One young woman dipped her pot in the spring and put the pot on her head to walk back to her hut. But as she passed, the man glared scowlingly at her and she broke into a run. To him, this was a sign of guilt and he leaped to his feet to pursue her. Strangely, she did not even remove the water pot from her head as she ran as fast as she could.

But the vengeful man was faster. Running up behind her he swung the large machete with all the power he possessed. The blade struck the back of her neck and all but severed her head from her body! She fell face down and he immediately slashed off both her hands, thrust the stump of each wrist in his mouth and sucked the blood! Then, rising to his feet, he spat on her, wiped the blood from his machete on her body, and walked back to his hut. He had been avenged.

Strangely, many of the people of the village saw nothing wrong in his actions. After all, the young woman should not have killed the man's wife by putting a curse upon her!

The last we heard, the government officials had taken the man into custody.

The Sorrow of Hopelessness

First Thessalonians 4:13 says, ***"But I would not have you to be ignorant, brethren, concerning them which are asleep, that ye sorrow not, even as others which have no hope. "***

One day Dr. Carl Becker and I walked to a native village. Just as we approached the mud huts, we were startled by the piercing shrieks of several voices in one of the little grass-topped houses. A man and several women came dashing out the door, yelling, wailing, and sobbing as they did so. The blood-curdling screams had scared me half to death and I stopped still in my tracks and watched in amazement and horror. They ran aimlessly back and forth and around and around, occasionally throwing themselves to the ground and rolling over and over as if in great agony. The man, with his fists, beat himself on the back of the head. The women pounded themselves on their legs or clawed at their faces and breasts.

I wondered what in the world was going on. The piercing screams, the loud sobbing, the wailing, and the frenzied, aimless running scared me.

I turned to my companion and said, "Dr. Becker, what in the world is the matter with these folks?"

Very solemnly the missionary doctor replied, "A woman has just died. That man was her husband and these other women are also his wives. I did everything I could for her, but I thought she would probably die today."

After a moment's pause he added, "Bill, you are seeing the sorrow of those who have no hope."

The most tragic thing in all the world is the death of one who dies without Christ. He has no hope of Heaven, and his loved ones have no hope of ever seeing him again.

New Creatures in Christ Jesus

But what a change the Lord Jesus Christ makes! Even in blackest Africa the lives of Christians are completely different than those of the unsaved.

Christian parents do not think of a baby girl as something that will, later on, bring them "wealth" when she is sold to a husband. They do not think of a baby boy as one who may furnish them a meal ticket in later years. Instead, like good Christians around the world, they feel that it is a privilege and a responsibility to *"...* *bring them up in the nurture and admonition of the Lord."*

A wife is no longer a possession little higher than another beast of burden but is a beloved companion and helpmate. Believe me, every woman on earth ought to fall on her knees and thank God for Jesus Christ! Where Christ is not preached, women are vassals. It is only where Jesus Christ is preached and accepted that women become one with their husbands.

Lives are changed. Those who once indulged in heathen rites now joyfully participate in gospel services.

Even the ceremonies of death are far different for the Christian than for his unsaved neighbor.

During the Amstutz revival, an old woman who had been a Christian for many years, died. Now, as a rule, the tribe to which she belonged buried the dead by digging a round hole four or five feet into the ground and then at the bottom of the hole, excavating a little room at one side. The dead body would be placed in this little side excavation, sitting up, knees drawn up, and head bent over. Then the round hole would be filled with earth, leaving the body sitting up in a tiny cave beneath the ground.

But when this Christian woman died, the natives wanted her to be honored in her burial. They borrowed the missionary's cross-cut saw and sawed planks out of tree trunks. With these planks they fashioned a coffin. It had cracks in it and was heavy as lead—but it was a coffin. They placed the body of the old woman in it, dug a grave on the slope of the mountain, and buried her there.

I was requested to bring the funeral message and did so in the falling rain.

I read, with Harold Amstutz interpreting, the story of The Creation. I explained that in just six days God had made the earth and everything in it. In just six days God had made the mountains. He had made the great jungles, He had made *bodi*, the deer, and *simba*, the lion, *timbu*, the elephant, *makako*, the monkey, and finally *Adomi*, the man, and *Eva*, the woman.

Then I read John 14:1-3 and explained that Jesus had gone back to Heaven almost two thousand years ago to build a home for us. I then said—incidentally—that if God had made the earth and everything on it in just six days, think how wonderful Heaven must be now that Jesus has been working on it for almost two thousand years. With me it had been almost a chance remark. But to those who heard, it was overwhelmingly wonderful! It was the favored subject of conversation during the rest of that revival. I think many of the older Christians envied the one who had died and who had gone to be in a house that had taken God Himself almost two thousand years to build.

Clothing, it seemed to me, was worn more for style than for covering or protection. Nakedness, to most Africans that I saw, was simply a way of life and they took it matter-of-factly. However, I saw very few men or women who did not at least wear a string tied around the hips that sustained a little apron or loincloth. The only exceptions were the Lotukas, perhaps the most savage tribe in Africa, and the Dinkas, the tallest tribe of people on earth. Many, many men of this tribe are seven feet tall and skinny as a fence post!

Men of the Dinka tribe are street cleaners in the little city of Juba. It looked so strange to me to see finely dressed Belgian officials sharing the dusty street with the tall, skinny, completely naked Dinkas!

3

THE JUNGLE KILLER

With a Beautiful Body But an Evil Heart, the African Leopard Is Treacherous—Never to Be Trusted

Spots as Dangerous as Dice

The leopard may be found in more places than any of the other great jungle cats. He may be found today in Europe, east of the Black Sea, in Southern Asia, China, Java, Sumatra, Malaya, Ceylon, and all of Africa except the Sahara Desert.

Pound for pound he is just about the fightingest critter in all the world. Leopards grow larger in Africa, for some reason or other, than any other place in the world. A real large male will weigh about 200 pounds and will be a little better than eight feet long from the tip of his nose to the tip of his tail. In other words, the largest leopard will be about the size of the smallest lion.

Many Africans fear the leopard more than any other beast of the jungle. The lion, rhinoceros, buffalo, elephant, and gorilla are dangerous; but they do not compare with the leopard for combined

31

cunning, boldness, speed, killing ability, and just plain downright cussedness.

In most places the leopard is regarded as a pest. Many even put a bounty on his head. They sometimes become man-killers. More often, however, they are hated because they are destructive thieves.

All leopards are spotted. Occasionally there are black leopards or "black panthers." A black leopard is still spotted and is still a leopard. The color is just a phase of the typical leopard.

Many believe that the black leopard is more vicious than his spotted brother. Whether this is true or superstition, the natives in Africa certainly fear him more.

Like many animals, the leopard has an amazing ability to conceal himself in almost any surrounding. Unlike most other wild animals, however, the leopard does not try to avoid human beings. Again and again, they have been known to enter native villages at night, slink along in the shadows on the prowl for dogs, goats, chickens and even, on occasions, native children.

A missionary in the Congo told me how a leopard visited him one night. He was sleeping in a mud house when a leopard jumped lightly in through the window. Old "Spot" walked between the cots on which the missionary and a companion were sleeping and slipped around the room. When he brushed against a table and knocked a water bucket off, the clatter seemed to frighten him and he jumped back through the window and disappeared.

Death to the Doggy

One night, I was in the mission station of Harold and Jane Amstutz. When missionaries first went to the Congo they usually built the mission stations on top of the highest hills. They felt that the higher they were the safer they would be from malaria-bearing mosquitoes. The idea was a good one except for the fact that—like so many of mine—it just didn't work! But many of the stations were started on the mountain tops and remain there 'til this day.

I was in a revival with the Amstutzes and they put me in a mud house with a thatched roof.

We sent runners out to tell the natives about the revival meetings. "Come," the runner said, "see a tall man who came across the waters in a big bird. He has a message from God to you!"

There were five services a day and approximately five thousand people per service. God gave many wonderful conversions.

It was interesting to me to see these people come from all around that neck of the woods. Men came with their wives, their children, and their dogs.

Of course, I was interested in the dogs these natives had. Some were mongrels of all descriptions. But some had dogs that were peculiar, I understand, to Africa. They were slick-hair dogs with big eyes and that did not bark. I was told that they actually cried tears when they were hurt. Unlikely as this sounds, I have since read articles about these dogs that seem to bear out the fact that they really cannot bark and that they really do cry tears!

Anyway—one night after the meetings were over the Amstutzes, the Austin Pauls and I were enjoying coffee and cookies under the stars. As we visited, we noticed a skinny, yellow dog walking toward us. The dog had all the earmarks of a stray. As he walked between the mud huts, he looked first one way and then another.

"His master will be looking for him pretty soon," Harold Amstutz said. "Otherwise, a leopard will get him sure before the night is over."

When I left the others to go to my room, I noticed the dog still walking about. "Don't you reckon I better take that dog to my room for the night?" I asked.

"No," Harold replied. "His master is bound to be looking for him and he wouldn't know where to find him. Don't worry about him, that dog will be all right."

I went on to my room, prayed for awhile, wrote Cathy a letter and finally, past midnight, went to bed. I had just begun to doze off when right outside my door was a snarl, a *thud*, a gasp and then an awful scream. *A leopard had caught that dog!*

I reached under my pillow for a flashlight, jumped out of my bed, sprang across the room to where my gun belt was hanging on the back of a chair, jerked a .357 Magnum six-gun from its holster, and rushed to the door. But I was too late. Even as I was moving, the screams began speeding away from my door. The leopard had circled my hut and in great leaps was running down the side of the mountain. I peered into the darkness but could see nothing. I could only hear the agonized screams of that poor dog as he was carried away. When the leopard reached the foot of the mountain the screams ceased as suddenly as they had begun. Heartsick, I went back to my hut and to my bed. This time I put the six-shooter under my pillow along with the flashlight.

Austin Paul's Pie-wagon

My next encounter with a leopard was of a more personal nature. In fact, you might say it was downright intimate. We met a big black one who was a strong believer in integration between leopards and people.

But before I tell you about that adventure, I must say a word about Austin Paul's Pie-wagon. It was a Metro and they are used in our cities every day to deliver milk, cakes, pies, bread, etc. It is a panel truck with a sliding door on either side. On the driver's side there is a wheel and a folding chair. On the other side is the engine. It is arranged so that the driver can step out either door quickly and easily to make deliveries.

Mr. Paul had rigged his up more like a bus with a narrow center aisle and seats on either side for about eight people with space for luggage at the rear. Mr. Paul always drove and I sat on the seat right across from him. We usually drove with the sliding doors open and I would put my feet up on the engine in front of me.

The sliding door on my side was sprung and it usually took two men and a boy to either open or close it.

Mrs. Paul, surely one of the greatest missionary women who ever lived, always went with us. She rode in the seat right behind *Bwana* Paul. Then the four natives who made up the brass quartet were always with us, too. They sprawled out in the rear seats.

Midnight on the Road to Rethy

We were on the road to Rethy. It was past midnight. All of us were bone tired. The four natives were snoring away peacefully in the back of the Pie-wagon. *Bwana* Paul, Mrs. Paul, and I had been talking about first one thing and then another. As usual, I was sprawled lazily in my seat with my long legs propped up on the engine. We were talking about the conferences the next day that would begin for the missionaries of A.I.M. They would be coming, *Bwana* Paul told me, from all over the Congo, from the Sudan, and from Ugandi. They met every other year and I had been invited to come as their speaker.

We were driving down a "road" that was really a widened game trail. The road led through a forest of giant trees, tangled vines, and dense vegetation.

Suddenly, a black shape jumped from an overhanging limb in the center of the road.

"It's a black leopard," I yelled as I reached for the powerful Magnum six-gun in its holster on the seat beside me.

The great cat was bounding down the road ahead of the Pie-wagon. It moved in great graceful leaps.

I leaned through the door and pulled the trigger without taking time to aim. With a loud screaming snarl, the black cat turned head over heels in the road.

I had hit him a terrific wallop.

When the cat screamed, *Bwana* Paul hit the brakes, bringing the car to a jerking, jolting, screeching halt. The sleeping natives were thrown from their seats. What happened next sounds like something from "I Love Lucy!" You would think that any beast hit with a Magnum slug would either die or escape into the jungle. But this cotton pickin' kitty did neither. Instead, with a roar of rage and pain, he bounded to his feet, flattened his ears down against his skull, opened his mouth, and came back on a dead run. I thought at first he was a crazy, mixed-up cat that just didn't know which way he was going. But I soon changed my mind. This baby obviously believed in tit for tat, an eye for an eye, and a hind end for a hind end!

As he headed for us, I pulled the trigger and the big gun boomed again. I saw the dust kick up in the road. I pulled again and missed again. Twice more I pulled the trigger and missed both times.

By now this had become the noisiest place on the entire continent of Africa. Outside was the snarling, screaming rage of the black panther. Inside, four terrified natives were all—honest to goodness—lying down in that small center aisle. They were all hollering their heads off. Their eyes in the darkness looked like fried eggs in a skillet! And—each one was trying to crawl under everybody else!

I dropped the gun and tried to close the sliding door. Naturally, it wouldn't budge!

The mayhem-minded cat was now just in front of the truck and still coming at full speed. In another moment he would be inside the Pie-wagon ready for revenge and supper.

I felt sure he would start with vanilla!

I wondered if I would have a chance of crawling under all four of my black friends who were trying to crawl under each other.

Wishing I could swap places with the knot-head who made doors that did not work in an emergency, I again grabbed the six-shooter and leaned from the truck.

As I did so the jungle killer, still squalling up a storm, had arrived. He was so close I could almost have kissed him—if he had been more my type!

I fired point blank and this time I did not miss. I hit him so solidly that he was knocked backward off his feet. As I reached for my second pistol he dragged himself out of the road into the jungle.

"Man alive!" I gasped as I sat back in my seat.

The four black boys began getting to their feet and edging forward to look through the door.

Then I looked over at the Pauls. Neither one of them had budged a single inch.

Mrs. Paul smiled and calmly said, "My, that was exciting, wasn't it!"

You know what Austin Paul said? He said, "I'm going to fix that door one of these days when I get around to it!"

The Danger of a Dying Leopard

We could tell the location of the wounded jungle cat by his heavy breathing. He dragged himself about fifteen feet into the jungle and stopped. There he was—no further away than across an average size room. We sat, without talking, in the Pie-wagon. We were just listening. In five or six minutes the breathing stopped.

We strained our ears but could not hear a thing except the night noises of the jungle.

"He's dead," I said as I drew a small camp knife. "Where's the flashlight?"

Austin Paul asked me what I was going to do and I said I was going to drag the dead cat into the road and skin it.

"No, you're not," *Bwana* Paul said. "It was pretty small but, of course, it might have been a female leopard. It could tear out a man's entrails with just one slash of a paw and many a dying leopard has come to life just long enough to kill a hunter. You would be risking your life foolishly to go into the jungle after him tonight."

A few minutes later we were bouncing down the road on the way to Rethy.

Past Sins Are a Dying Leopard

Stay away from sin—it is as dangerous as a dying leopard. II Corinthians 5:17 says, *"Therefore if any man be in Christ, he is a new creature; old things are passed away; behold, all things are become new."*

God wants those who are saved to *"...walk in newness of life."*

Even though saved, we still have the same bodies and the old nature.

It would be foolish for one who has been a drunkard before his conversion to hang around saloons after he has been saved.

It would be foolish for one who has lived an adulterous life before his conversion to continue running around with the same wicked companions after his conversion.

Sin Is Always Dangerous

Romans 6:11 says, *"Likewise reckon ye also yourselves to be dead indeed unto sin...."*

That is, leave sin alone!

Colossians 3:5 says, *"Mortify therefore your members which are upon the earth; fornication, uncleanness, inordinate affection, evil concupiscence, and covetousness, which is idolatry."*

Verse 7 goes on to say that there was a time when we lived in sin but now we have *"...put on the new man, which is renewed in knowledge after the image of him that created him."*

Good Neighbor, sin is always dangerous. It is like a dying leopard.

4

HUNTING WILD ELEPHANTS

The Chase…An Elephant Throws a Warrior for a Forward Pass…The Bravery of the Commandant…The Capture…The Ropes of Sin

It must have been about three o'clock in the black morning of the African tropics when I stepped out of my candle-lit room. By invitation of the Belgian king, I had come to his huge ranch in the heart of the Congo to go on an elephant hunt.

Out in the courtyard, in the light of a dozen flickering torches, I could see three white men and a hundred natives standing around a crude wooden table. They were preparing for the day's hunt. In the weird torchlight the black bodies of the warriors gleamed mysteriously as they moved in and out of the shadows.

These men were not only warriors but expert hunters, and they were making preparation for the dangerous and exciting events that would take place that day. Some of these men were coiling long lengths of large handmade rope. Others, squatting on their heels, were cleaning ancient Army rifles. On one edge of the group a dozen men were harnessing and tying equipment on several huge elephants. On the opposite side of the circle other warriors were holding eight horses that had already been bridled and saddled. As I approached the group, one of the white men came to meet me with a big smile on his face and his hand outstretched in greeting. He was Captain LeFever, the Commandant of the Army outpost and manager of the king's ranch. He was a slender young man dressed in an Army uniform consisting of a pith tropic helmet, short-sleeved khaki military shirt, and wearing shorts and boots!

He was a dandy fellow and I sure did like him. Although he spoke nothing but French and I spoke nothing but Texan, we greeted each other with a warm handshake and a slap on the shoulder as he led me to the table and motioned me to help myself to strong black coffee and fruit juice.

Just then the two white missionaries who had accompanied me to the ranch came walking up out of the darkness. We exchanged greetings, bowed our heads for a brief word of prayer, and then turned to the coffee and fruit juice.

The coffee was not only scalding hot but was strong and so bitter that I just couldn't go it. The fruit juice, though, was delicious and I drank a couple of tin cups of it.

Hippos in the River

By the time we were finished with coffee and fruit juice, the natives had quickly packed their gear and had lined up in a double column for the march.

Captain LeFever led me over to the horses and indicated that I was to ride a red roan stallion. Through an interpreter (one of the missionaries), Captain LeFever told me that the horse's name was *Bonga* (A Horn) and that he was the second best horse the king owned in Africa. I assured the commandant that it was a great honor to ride such a noble animal, and began adjusting the stirrups for my long legs.

In a few moments we were mounted and, at the captain's call, brawny blacks with torches held over their heads marched out of the camp. We followed on our horses and the double column of natives, carrying rope, food, water, ammunition, and other gear, followed us. Other natives on the huge elephants brought up the rear. Two of my white companions rode on the elephants behind the native drivers who sat on the elephants' heads.

It was so dark I could scarcely see a thing, but when we had ridden about half a mile I realized that the trail had begun to slant downward. In a few minutes we came to a river that must have been about one hundred yards across. When the warriors in the lead came to the edge of the river they stopped, holding their torches high above their heads. Presently, one of them stepped into the water, whirled his torch around his head a couple of times, and then threw it far out over the black water. As the burning torch shot out into an arc, I saw big black bumps dotting the surface of the water.

At first I thought they were stumps until they began to submerge as the torch fell—and I realized I was not looking at stumps but at the heads of hippopotami as they glared at us and then submerged.

The torchbearers hesitated but a moment and then began wading out into the dark waters. I felt sorry for them for a moment, but then the commandant motioned me to follow him as he urged his horse into the river. After that, I felt sorry for myself! Behind me the long line of warriors silently waded into the waters, holding their guns and packs above their heads.

As the water swirled around the knees and then the flanks of my horse, I crossed my ankles in front of the saddle horn to keep my boots from being filled with water.

Not a man said a word as we silently crossed the stream. At the edge of the light from the torches we could see, here and there, heads of the awesome water beasts appearing and submerging. The hippopotami did not bother any of us, however, and we crossed the river without mishap. I think all of us breathed a sigh of relief when we began wading out of the water onto the dry sand on the other bank of the river.

Bonga, the Red Roan Stallion

The horse I was riding was a small one. In fact, all of the horses were pony-size. Moreover, all of them were so skinny you could hang your hat on their hips and count just about every rib.

Bonga held his head at a dispirited downward angle, plodding along as though he were a hundred years old and carried the burden of the world on his skinny back. He didn't look to the right nor to the left but was totally without interest in anything as far as I could tell. Once or twice we broke into a trot and he was as rough as a corncob!

Because the captain had been told I was an expert horseman he had selected this mount for me, carefully explaining that this was the second best horse available. I felt the captain surely must be a half-wit or a liar because there simply couldn't be eight horses in the entire Congo worse than this one. If I ever in my life saw a horse that was just plain crow-bait, this was the one!

As we moved silently along, the darkness of the night turned to gray, then to golden dawn, and then into bright sunlight. We were going through the bush—plains dotted with dwarfed trees. We saw any number of deer and one giraffe. The giraffe was taller than the tree he was feeding upon. We must have ridden silently along for a hundred yards or more before the giraffe spotted us. But when he saw us he turned tail and ran to beat sixty. I was amazed at the speed with which he ran in and out among the trees and disappeared in the distance.

It must have been about ten o'clock in the morning when one of the advance scouts came running back to report that he had discovered elephant spoor (manure). The procession was halted while one of the natives, finding a fairly tall tree, quickly climbed it to look around. Presently he came down and told us that we had gone past a large herd of elephants but, fortunately, we had been downwind of them and so they had not detected our presence.

The Chase

Quickly the warriors spread out in a semicircle with the commandant riding back and forth, whispering last-minute instructions. Some of the natives carried large coils of ropes and others carried rifles.

The strategy was very simple. The men with the rifles were to "charge," firing their guns in the air in an effort to scare the elephants into a stampede. Theoretically, the older, larger elephants would run off from the younger ones. Then the men with the ropes would be able to catch up with the young elephants and lasso them.

I had already been told that when the chase began I was to ride one hundred yards behind the captain. I was unarmed and he carried two small revolvers on bandoleers beneath each armpit.

The men crept slowly through the bush toward the elephant herd. No one made a sound until a giant bull elephant either heard or saw us. Leaving the herd he came toward us, stopped, put his great ears out like fans, and held his trunk high in the air.

Suddenly that trunk came down and pointed straight at us and we knew we had been spotted.

At the captain's command all of the warriors jumped to their feet, yelled at the top of their voices, fired the rifles, and ran toward the herd of elephants.

There must have been some two hundred elephants in the bunch. For just a moment they seemed undecided as to whether they would fight or run. Then fear got the better of many of them and they turned tail and stampeded. The great bulls who seemed willing to fight reluctantly turned and followed. These big fellows, however, did not panic as they had been expected to do; and this almost caused the death of several men, including the captain.

Overtaking Danger

Elephants—even the larger ones—are not very fast animals. But they are so large and heavy that they can run right through tall grass and over bushes without being slowed down in the least. I believe that the average African warrior could outrun the average grown elephant. At least for a short distance. And they can certainly outrun half-grown and baby elephants. So when the herd stampeded, men with ropes began overtaking the younger elephants. It looked as though the warriors were going to have a record-breaking hunt as they closed in on a number of the youngsters.

As soon as the chase began, that little red roan stallion I was riding suddenly came to life. He was an old hand at this business and evidently he loved it. He began to rear and plunge and fight for his head. Before I knew it the crazy thing had zipped past the men on foot and it was he and I who were closing in on the elephants! Now, I don't think I'm a sissy but Austin Paul and I had been charged by one bull elephant that had already killed two men—and I did not want an encounter with another. I was trying to get this idea across to *Bonga*, but he didn't get the message until I whacked him between the ears a couple of times and managed to calm him down.

Even so, I apologized to that little red horse for everything mean I had been thinking about him. He really was a dandy! The line of men had now spread about a quarter of a mile as different groups selected various elephants to chase and try to capture. I had the time of my life riding *Bonga* in a dead run from one group to the other. He jumped fallen trees, gullies, and bushes. He was so sure-footed he never stumbled one single time and he seemed to have unusual stamina and fleetness. Before the ride was over I wondered if there could possibly be a better horse than this in all the Congo!

The herd of elephants seemed frightened except, you will remember, for several large bulls that did not panic and seemed ready to fight.

As I was riding toward one small group of warriors that was closing in on a young elephant, I saw two large bulls come charging out of the bush to meet them. The two groups almost collided but the warriors turned and scattered in every direction. To my horror, I saw the two big bulls overtake one of the half-naked natives. He was turning and twisting to elude the elephant but to no avail. I heard the man scream as the two elephants closed in on him. My horse was fairly flying as I turned him toward the man and the two elephants.

Even as my horse wheeled I saw one of the elephants throw his trunk around the frightened man's waist. I saw the elephant swing the native high above his head and then throw him, still screaming, through the air like a football player making a forward pass!

The poor man, twisting and turning, sailed through the air for what seemed to be an incredible length of time. It was almost like watching in slow motion. And then he hit the ground with a thud. Instantly the two elephants were upon him again. Trying to run their long ivory tusks through him, the elephants literally plowed up the ground as the screaming man wriggled and turned and twisted frantically beneath them.

The Captain to the Rescue

I felt sure he was doomed as I raced toward him, wondering all the time what in the world I would do when I got there! It turned out, however, that I did nothing—the captain got there first. I had not even seen him but there he was, riding straight up to the giant beasts, firing his small revolvers!

The elephants immediately left their victim to charge the horse and rider. Then and there I witnessed one of the bravest acts I have ever seen in all my life. I saw Captain LeFever deliberately hold his horse in until the elephants were within a few feet of him. The horse was so frightened he was rearing and plunging to get away. If the captain had been thrown or if the rearing, plunging horse had fallen with him, I think it would have meant instant death. When the elephants were almost upon him, he gave the horse some rein and let him gallop slowly away, just barely keeping out of reach of the elephants until he had led them away from the stricken man.

It scared me half to death because the captain headed straight for me. I whirled *Bonga* and presently we gave the horses their heads and quickly outdistanced the elephants. Then, side by side, we rode back to the warrior who was still lying on the ground.

(Oddly enough, although the man was badly bruised and beaten, he did not have a bone broken nor, as far as we could tell, even a cut or bad scratch! But the last time I saw him—two days later—he was still shaking as though in a nervous chill.)

A Second Rescue

While other warriors picked the injured man up and carried him back out of the way, the captain and I galloped back after the fleeing elephant herd. We were going up a little incline when suddenly, in front of us, a native dashed out of the bush heading straight for us. And right behind him was history repeating itself! I'll declare if he wasn't being chased by a great bull elephant!

This time, however, the elephant did not catch the man. The captain quickly spurred his horse between the native and the elephant; and again the great beast followed the horse and rider, trying in vain to catch them. Again the valiant captain had saved a life at the risk of losing his own. It's a wonder his horse didn't have a nervous breakdown right then and there. Come to think of it—it's a wonder I didn't have a couple of breakdowns myself!

The Capture

This time the captain and I were separated and I went on alone, urging my horse into a dead run to overtake the running men and elephants. In a couple of minutes I came upon several men on foot who had separated a young elephant from the herd and were trying to capture him. I had wondered how they got those big ropes on the elephants and now I found out.

I saw a giant of a man, with a large coil of rope around his shoulder, running along behind an elephant. And I do mean right behind. The man's shoulder was pushing against the elephant's rump! And as the two of them ran, the man took the coil of rope from his shoulder and reaching down, passed the rope around one of the elephant's hind legs. Still running, he began tying the rope around the elephant's leg.

All the time I was galloping along beside the man, watching the entire operation.

When the big native had the rope tied around the elephant's leg, he suddenly stopped and tied the other end of the rope around a small tree and jerked the elephant to a stop. The big beast was only captured for a moment, however, for he immediately broke the rope. But the brief delay gave other men time to spread loops on the ground around the elephant and it stepped into one of them. Now he was caught again. Some of the men tied the end of their ropes to a small tree and to my surprise, the elephant dashed over, wrapped his trunk around the tree, pulled it up by the roots, and ran off carrying it like Samson with the gates of Gaza!

A warrior in his path was knocked sprawling.

But the men quickly caught hold of the ropes again and new ropes were added. The elephant struggled but to no avail. He was not only tired fighting, but there were too many ropes now for him to break. He could break one rope, or two—but not twenty.

Presently other warriors came riding up on the great tame elephants and quickly ended the struggle. These big elephants got on either side of the captured youngster and squeezed him tightly in between them while the warriors tied the captive securely to the two tame elephants.

Soon they had started the long journey back to headquarters with the captive.

The Ropes of Sin

I had witnessed the struggle and capture from the back of a very uneasy little stallion. As I saw one rope after another fastened to the half-grown elephant, it seemed to me I was watching a sermon against sin. The elephant could break one rope but the one led to another and another until there were too many for him to escape.

So people are so often captured by little sins.

I have talked with many a teenager who felt there couldn't be any real danger in just one little drink of beer. Or just one dance. Or just going to the movies one time. Or stealing just one little object.

But there is harm—great harm—in doing something wrong just once. One sin, you see, leads to two sins. And two leads to three.

After all, there never was a drunkard who did not begin with just one drink. Now, I have never in my life talked to a drunkard who would not give anything in all the world if only he had never taken that first drink. But he *did* take that first drink because he thought it would be fun and did not dream it would lead to a life of sin and shame that would ruin his own chances for happiness and break the hearts of everyone who loved him.

And, make no mistake about it, sin and shame can be the result of just one dance or petting party. I have counseled with pregnant girls all over the country who simply would not listen to parents or pastors or friends or counselors about the danger of dancing or petting. They were determined, it seems, to find out the hard way that there simply aren't any harmless sins. One sin may well lead to a ruined life.

I remember talking one time to a group of teenage boys in jail. They were part of a band of car thieves. But in talking with them, I discovered that they had never intended to steal a car when they first began. They just stole some gas, then hub caps, then spare tires and—finally—an automobile. Prison was the result of stealing just one little thing! Great sins always come from little ones.

Four elephants were captured that day. They were all captured the very same way. Natives managed to get one rope around them and that one rope slowed them down enough that they could get other ropes on them.

And one sin may slow you down enough for the Devil to capture you completely.

That's What the Bible Says

This is the teaching of the very first Psalm. The very first verse says, **"Blessed is the man that walketh not in the counsel of the ungodly, nor standeth in the way of sinners, nor sitteth in the seat of the scornful."**

Do you notice that people first *walk* around sinful people, then *stand* around them, and then *sit down* with them? This is the progression of sin. Walking—standing—sitting.

There never was anyone who could sin and get by with it.

"Be sure your sin will find you out."—*Numbers 32:23b.*

"Be not deceived; God is not mocked: for whatsoever a man soweth, that shall he also reap."—*Galations 6:7.*

"Sin, when it is finished, bringeth forth death."—*James 1:15b.*

Young fellow—do right!

Little lady—do right!

Do not go into sin at all. Don't take a chance. Give your heart and life to Jesus Christ today and live for Him. If you are already in the clutches of sinful habits that will ruin your life, damn your soul, and break the hearts of everyone who loves you—turn to Christ. Ask Him to forgive you and save you and He will!

Romans 6:23 says, **"The wages of sin is death; but the gift of God is eternal life through Jesus Christ our Lord."**

By all means trust Christ as your Lord and Saviour and—do it right now!

5

THE DEATH OF A CHIEF

Thirty-five Hundred Warriors in a Frenzied Dance That Would Climax in Drunkenness, Blood and Lust

It was almost high noon. The Congo sun was high in the heavens, hot, and glaring bright.

Inside the pie-wagon type delivery truck, Austin Paul was driving and he and Mrs. Paul and I were lazily talking. I remember I had my long legs stretched out until my booted feet were resting on the engine. The four Christian natives who helped us in the meetings were sprawled out in the rear seats, dreamily looking out the windows or dozing. We had really been hitting the ball in the last revival campaign with five services daily and approximately five thousand people attending each service.

We were not due to begin our next revival until that night, and since the drive was not a long one, we were taking our own sweet time. Right now we were looking for a place to stop and eat our lunch.

A Dusty African Road

The dusty road we were following was hardly more than a trail. As we had driven along the last few miles, we had not seen the usual number of native men, women, and children. And we had vaguely wondered where everyone was. Now, however, we began passing natives in increasing numbers along the trail.

"Notice anything peculiar about these natives we are passing?" Austin Paul asked me.

I looked at them more closely but did not notice anything out of the ordinary. Some of the women wore a sarong, while others were naked except for a grass skirt. Many of the smaller boys and girls were completely naked, while most of the girls in their early teens wore grass skirts and most of the boys of the same age wore ragged trousers of one kind or another. It was a hot day and little rivers of sweat ran down their dust-covered bodies.

After a bit I said to *Bwana* Paul, "I do notice one thing—all these folks are going in the same direction."

"That's right," *Bwana* said, "but do you notice something else that is even more peculiar—there are no men on the trail today. There are just women and children."

Now that I noticed it, this was true. Except for an occasional old fellow, there were no men on the trail. Just women and children.

We wondered where in the world they were going. I suggested they might be going to a market, but *Bwana* Paul quickly pointed out that they were not carrying anything to sell or trade. Then perhaps, I suggested, they were going to a party. But Mrs. Paul quickly put the kibosh on this idea. "Never," she snorted. "If there was work to be done you might see the women without any men around. But any time there is playing or feasting or festivities of any kind you will see men whether you see any women or not."

"Oh, I don't know," *Bwana* said, "maybe men have gone on ahead and these are the ones that just couldn't keep up!"

As it turned out, *Bwana Smarty* was exactly one hundred percent correct. This wisecrack of his hit the nail square on the thumb!

The Man in the Dunce Cap

Suddenly we saw one of the strangest characters I have ever seen in all my life. A black man came running toward us from a side trail and he entered the main road right even with us. Austin Paul slowed the Pie-wagon down so that we kept pace with him.

This man was a large, powerfully-built fellow. He was as black as a man could possibly be. He was covered with sweat and dust, but it was his costume that held us absolutely spellbound.

On his head there was a hat that looked for all the world like a dunce's cap. It was a cone-shaped straw hat, but it must have been at least three feet tall. It was tied with a string beneath his chin and on the very tip of the hat there were white feathers from an egret.

Around his neck there were several strings of beads. One was made of leopard's teeth, another was made of some kind of seeds, and another was bits of colored glass.

Long strands of grass or dried moss were tied to either elbow and, as the man ran, these strands of grass flowed out behind like streamers.

Except for a brief skin loincloth, the man was naked. Little bells, like those found on a baby's rattle, were suspended from a belt around his waist. Narrow strips of leather, like fringe, hung from the loincloth. A buffalo tail hung from each hip.

It seemed obvious he had been running for some distance. His mouth was open and his breath seemed to come in huffs and puffs. He did not run lightly but rather trotted with a *thud, thud, thud*. He was a powerfully-built man and the muscles of his chest, arms, and legs rippled beneath his black skin.

"*Senna minge*, " I howdy-ed.

"*Senna minge, Bwana*," he grunted back.

In *Bangala* tongue Austin Paul called out, asking where he was going. The man grunted a reply and, after this brief conversation, *Bwana* stepped on the gas; and we were again sailing along at the tremendous speed of about twenty miles an hour!

I asked Mr. Paul what the man had said and he answered that he knew what the fellow had said but did not know what the fellow meant. He had said the big chief had died and he was going to dance at the funeral!

It turned out that this statement was just a little misleading. The fact was, the great chief had died approximately a year ago and this was a celebration to honor the dead chief for the mighty deeds he had done.

The Death Dance

Ahead of us, on an open prairie, there was a great crowd of people. As we drove up we saw one of the strangest sights any man has ever seen on the African continent.

The great crowd covered several acres of ground. The fringe of the crowd was composed of hundreds and hundreds of women and children. Some were dancing, some clapped their hands, many of them singing a weird chant, some of them sitting on the ground, and others were lying down, sound asleep.

Small lean-tos dotted the scene and in their shade, old people sat or slept.

Inside this circle of women and children were some thirty-five hundred leaping, jumping, twisting, turning, screaming, chest-and-thigh-beating, semi-nude warriors dancing....

They were dressed like the oddball character we had met running on the trail. Imagine thousands of men wearing those tall dunce-like straw hats with white feathers streaming from the peak. Some of them had greased their bodies with palm fat and they glistened like polished ebony in the bright sunlight.

Every man seemed to have a real or miniature weapon in his hand. Most of them carried war axes, but a few had spears and some had wicked-looking, longbladed fighting knives.

There was little or no going back and forth through the great crowd. Most of the men danced back and forth in almost the same spot—a few steps forward, a few back.

Near the outer edge of this great crowd were the drummers. Some were wooden drums played with sticks, but most of the drums were hollowed logs open at one end with skin stretched across the other and these were played like *Bongo* drums—by striking the palms of the hand against the head of the drum.

As the vast crowd danced, they sang a weird chant. It seemed the chant had only four notes, repeated over and over and over again. First a real high note, then one considerably lower, then one yet lower, and the fourth note yet lower.

We parked the Pie-wagon and *Bwana* Paul and I began walking toward what appeared to be a small canvas tent some distance away. We did not carry any guns at all, but I did tote a small camera on a strap around my neck and I carried my large movie camera and tripod in my arms.

We attracted very little attention as we made our way through the crowds of women and children. But the small tent was surrounded by a group of warriors armed with spears, and some of these men stepped forward to meet us. Austin Paul could speak their native tongue and from them we found out what the celebration was all about. A greatly-loved and admired chief had died some months before. Naturally, they had been forced to bury his body right away. But word had gone out throughout all the tribes to meet on this day to honor the dead chief. It really was a kind of a funeral service as well as a celebration. And, while they were about it, they would also meet the new chief. In fact, it was this new chief, the eldest son of the dead man, who was in the little tent surrounded by the spearmen.

Guests of the Fat Chief

We were ushered into the small tent to meet the oldest son of the late chief. He was a very fat young man. On his head was the tall straw hat with the white feather. Around his neck were several strands of leopard teeth. His loincloth was of leopard skin, denoting royalty. He was also wearing a thin, white undershirt with short sleeves. He was seated on a small stool and as we entered he was drinking from a can of beer. Empty beer cans littered the floor of the little tent.

He seemed flattered that white men were present on this great occasion; and when we told him we would like to walk through the great throng of dancers and take pictures, he not only agreed but offered to send members of his personal guard to help us make our way through the crowds. In fact, he walked a short distance with us into the crowd of dancers and stood by with half-closed eyes and expressionless face while I set up the movie camera. (We thought he was more than half-drunk.) Then, when I began taking moving pictures, he moved directly in front of the camera and began to dance. I have seen elephants that were hardly larger but a great deal more graceful!

Three Days of Dancing

As we moved further into the crowd, the fat chief turned and walked slowly back toward his tent.

The yelling was deafening—that peculiar four-note chant. As we made our way through the sweating, leaping, dancing men, we felt some of them keenly resented our presence. Some shook their battle axes in our faces and shouted for us to leave. When our honor guards explained that we were guests of the new chief they always gave way, although somewhat reluctantly, and we squeezed on through.

Finally, after perhaps forty-five minutes of struggle, we reached the middle of the dancers. Here we saw something new. One was a group of men dressed in leopard-skin loincloths. These, then, were members of the royal family—probably brothers of the new chief.

Here, too, were the only women in the vast circle of dancing men. These women—some young and some old—had their faces painted a startling white. They were the many widows of the dead chieftain. As they swayed to the beating of the drums and the chant of the dancers, they screamed and cried and beat their bodies to express their mourning for their dead husband.

Although there seemed to be a rather tense excitement among the several thousand dancers, there seemed to be no joy. There were no smiles, no laughter. In fact, it almost seemed that they danced under a hypnotic spell.

We signaled to our guards that we were ready to leave; and we slowly made our way through the howling, leaping, twisting dancers until finally, hot and tired and soaked with perspiration, we stood again at the edge of the great crowd. "How long," we asked the guards, "have these men been dancing?" To our surprise, we learned this was the third day! It would end sometime tonight. This was the third day the men had been dancing. They would dance, lie down for a quick nap, and then be on their feet to dance again. Most of them had fasted during the dance. But later tonight the dancing would end. It would come to a climax in an orgy of savage sin. After feasting, the men would spend the hours of darkness in bloody fighting, drunken drinking, and satisfying the appetites of fleshly lusts.

The savage wickedness of it all filled me with disgust as I walked away. One of the guards stopped me and said something in *Bangala*. I looked to Austin Paul for an interpretation. "He wants to know," *Bwana* Paul said; "if you ever celebrate the death of a great chief like this in your country."

"Tell him we certainly do not," I snapped as I made my way through the fringe crowd of women and children back toward the Pie-wagon.

The Death of Our Chief

But as we bumped along the dusty trail that afternoon, I suddenly realized how wrong I had been. Every year in America we celebrate the death, burial, and resurrection of a far greater chief—our Lord Jesus Christ. And yet, how does America celebrate His death? How do we in America remember the mighty deeds of the Saviour? How do we express our gratitude for what He has meant to us?

With deep shame I must admit that many of us here in America remember the death of Christ with the very same savage sin and shame, drunkenness and debauchery, lust and licentiousness, blood and brutality with which those thirty-five hundred warriors performed their death dance In memory of their deceased chief.

These African natives had not actually come to mourn their fallen chief nor to honor his memory for the great deeds he had done. They had simply taken his death as an occasion, an excuse for a drunken debauch.

And here in America multiplied thousands who despise the Lord Jesus Christ will, nevertheless, "celebrate" His death, burial, and resurrection. All over America at the Easter season there will be dances and wild parties featuring drunkenness and adultery.

Even Our Churches

Ironically enough, many sound, fundamental Bible churches that would not dream of desecrating Easter by such worldliness will dishonor Christ in an entirely different way. Many of these churches will have cute little Easter egg hunts for children, telling these youngsters cute little lies about the cute little rabbits that lay gaily-colored eggs at Easter time. Besides the fact that lying is morally wrong, there is an even greater sin in this. It is—as any publicity man knows—impossible to give two events equal importance. You simply cannot emphasize to a boy or girl that Jesus Christ died for our sins and was buried and rose again, and at the same time tell him that Easter is a time for bunny rabbits and Easter eggs. One of these two things will assume major importance at the expense of the other. And, sad to say, in many fundamental churches the big thing in the minds of our children at Easter time is not the resurrection of Christ but bunny rabbits and Easter eggs.

"Well hath Esaias prophesied of you hypocrites, as it is written, This people honoureth me with their lips, but their heart is far from me."—Mark 7:6.

6

THE LOTUKA SPEARMEN

Two Sick Missionaries and One Scared Evangelist and a War Party of Natives Who Had Reportedly Killed a Crew of English Well Diggers Only the Day Before

We conducted more revival campaigns in the Congo than in either the Sudan or Ugandi. But it was in the Sudan that we encountered native hatred for whites that spilled over the Nile as Mau Mau rebellion only a few weeks later.

The Egyptians had just begun an all-out attempt to get the British out. They had begun inciting the natives of the Sudan to rebel against the English.

As we were being ferried across the Nile River, I think we were vaguely aware that there was trouble brewing in the Sudan; but I don't believe it occurred to us that this trouble might affect us personally in any way.

We had left our guns in Juba because we expected to have little time for hunting and it was a bother to take them through customs on the border.

The Sudan

Natives here were as friendly as the natives we had met elsewhere in Africa. Christian natives especially were eager to show themselves friendly. For example, I mentioned one time I would like to take movies of some scorpions! They really had a collection for me! They had red ones, black ones, big and little ones. And, although it hurts me to say so, I do believe they were larger than the ones in Texas, which I heard of when I was a boy!

As usual, the missionaries were wonderful. Let me pause right here to say that the missionaries I met in Africa were the finest, cleanest, most dedicated group of soul winners you can imagine. I did and I do earnestly thank God for the privilege of being with them, and many are warm personal friends of mine today.

There was one elderly man I liked and admired very much. I do not know how to spell his name correctly but it was pronounced "Boys." He had reached the age of retirement and then had returned to spend one more term in Africa. His was one of the toughest assignments of any missionary. He had returned to try to gain a gospel foothold with the Lotuka Tribes, and when he invited *Bwana* Paul and me to go on a trip with him, we gladly accepted.

The Lotuka

The men of the Lotuka do not wear clothing of any kind. They go stark naked. When asked why they do not cover their nakedness they proudly answer, "We have nothing to hide," meaning they do not have social diseases. In this sense, they evidently do live unusually clean lives.

They are also very athletic. Many of the African natives are lazy and do little in the way of physical exercise. But the Lotuka love sporting events. They hold contests involving running, jumping, spear throwing, and—especially—wrestling. They take their wrestling seriously and, to my surprise, know most of the holds used by our TV fakers.

I said they took their wrestling seriously. They sure do! With heavy brass bracelets on their arms, they wrestle for prizes that sometimes include women they want for wives. As they struggle and strain, they are allowed to hit one another with their forearm and—remember—they are wearing those heavy bracelets! I was told that more than one suitor has been stretched out with a split skull!

Another unusual thing about the Lotuka is that they do not mix very much with other tribes or with whites. I was told that there was not a single white man in the whole world who could speak their language. What's more, because they were not only fighters but rather nomadic, they were the one tribe from whom the government never collected taxes.

These were the people an old man with white hair wanted to contact for Christ. He had seemingly made friends with some of them and had put up a mud hut with grass roof near some little mountains where the Lotuka often went to hunt.

The Camp

One fine morning we left the mission base in *Bwana* Paul's Pie-wagon. Four natives went with us. Two were helpers (cooks) of Mr. Boys and two were part of a quartet who always worked in revivals with Austin Paul.

Because there was no road, we were traveling light. We only carried our bed rolls and provisions for about a week. Austin drove and I sat in the right front seat with my feet propped up on the engine that was inside the cab. The going was rough but *Bwana* was an expert driver and we bounced across gullies, around trees, and over bumps without mishap. We reached camp in time for a good supper and devotions around the campfire before wearily turning in for the night.

The following morning we stayed around the camp without seeing anyone other than our own group. In the afternoon Mr. Boys, Mr. Paul, and I all three became sick. Mr. Boys suffered an acute attack of diarrhea and Austin Paul took some ayrlon tablets that made him sick. I had been suffering from malaria and was suddenly hit with fever, nausea, and a blinding headache.

By the following morning, *Bwana* Paul and I were both some better but Mr. Boys was not. About the middle of the morning, Mr. Boys was asleep and Mr. Paul was resting outside the hut. (The fact that he was *outside* may have saved my life a little later.) I had been vomiting every few minutes and felt weak—I was simply bushed.

Perhaps a half mile away I could see through the trees, the little mountains. Perhaps, I thought, it would be cooler there beneath the trees. (Besides, over there, I could regurgitate in privacy!) I decided to walk several hundred yards and find a spot to vomit, rest and pray.

Why I bothered to take my large motion picture camera with me I will never know, but I took it, tripod and all. The still camera was in a leather case attached to the tripod.

Beneath a large tree I set up the movie camera on the tripod and a bit later I was sitting on the ground leaning back against the tree. I was weak and felt sick thru and thru. Surely I would feel better after resting for awhile.

But there was to be no rest for me that day. I had hardly closed my eyes when I was startled by loud, shrill yelling from across the little clearing. I opened my eyes and then sat up in amazement. My first thought was that, in my fever, I was "seeing things." Racing toward me was a group of stark naked native spearmen!

The Warriors

In a nightmarish sort of way, the men were beautiful. Their black, naked bodies glistened in the sun because they had greased their bodies with palm oil. (In hand-to-hand fighting it makes their bodies slippery and harder for the opponent to hold.) They were lean and muscular and they moved with such grace they seemed almost to float across the grass as they came running toward me. Each man held one spear in his right hand in throwing position and two extra spears in his left hand.

Screaming, leaping—the sunlight dancing on their glistening bodies—they charged across the clearing.

I was startled but not scared. At that time we did not know of the brewing rebellion, did not know that there had already been bloodshed. (We later learned that these same men had helped "butcher" a crew of English well diggers the day before.) Most of the natives we had met in Congo, Ugandi, and the Sudan had been friendly and it did not enter my mind that these men were bent on mayhem. I just thought they were putting on some kind of a war dance for my entertainment.

I got to my feet, stepped behind the movie camera, swung it around, and began taking pictures of the spearmen.

As soon as I stepped behind the camera, the spearmen checked their forward run and darted to the right. They would dash to the right, then to the left, then drop to their knees, run backward a few paces and then circle again. But always they were coming closer. I remember thinking, "Man alive, what wonderful pictures! Just wait 'til the folks back home see this!"

The yelling, running, leaping, circling, ducking, and dodging went on…until I ran out of film. Then I stepped out in front of the camera and business began to pick up. It turned out that they had feared the camera was a gun. Now, warily, half walking, half trotting, they closed in. I said they were stark naked but one of them was not. One of them wore a hand-woven straw hat on his head! I rightly guessed that he was the chief.

As they approached I smiled and said, "*Senna Minge*," which means "hello" in *Bangala*. With stern faces, bodies bent in a crouch, they continued to come. "*Jambo*," I tried, which is "hello" in *Kingwana*. Still no response. Then "*Howdy*," which is "hello" in Texan. With grim faces they still advanced. I began to get uneasy. I was trying to say "hello" but these fellows looked more like "good-by!"

In fan-shaped formation they came on up until they were only six or eight feet away. I could have touched the points of their outstretched spears.

They had made no sound since I had stepped from behind the camera and they made no sound now. I still did not think they intended harming me but it was obvious they were unfriendly. I doubted they could understand a word of English, but wishing to look and sound friendly, I said, "Howdy, fellows—how y' doin'?"

For answer, the man on my right dropped the extra spears in his left hand, grabbed his other spear with both hands and lunged forward, aiming at my midsection!

Whew!!!

It was totally unexpected and I had no time to move except to flinch. I was wearing a cowboy belt and the point of that spear slid along the belt until it hit the buckle and was caught there.

"Great guns," I thought, "these guys intend to kill me!"

When the fellow lunged and his spear caught on my belt buckle, he whirled me partly around and fell against me, his shoulder against the back of my right shoulder. I immediately rammed my right elbow into his belly and it was his turn to be surprised. With a loud grunt he bent over almost double. When he did, I grabbed the head end of his spear with both hands and, pivoting upon my right foot, slammed it with all my might into his face. He went sailing backwards and was out of the fight.

I then did two of the smartest things any man could have done under the circumstances.

First, before the other warriors had time to attack, I turned to the fellow wearing the straw hat and grabbed him by the wrist as though to prevent him from running away. I rightly guessed that he was the chief and I yanked him toward me, slapped him across the chest with the back of my hand and yelled, "What in the world do you think you are doing?"

Now, I had never before in all my life hit a man with the *back* of my hand. It had never even occurred to me to do so. And I have never done it since. But, as it turned out, it doubtless saved my life. After all, there wasn't too much I could have done. I certainly could not have fought with even one of those warriors and come out alive. They were tremendous athletes and experienced fighters. And I dead sure couldn't have escaped by running. After all, how fast can even a scared feller run in cowboy boots!

But I could and I did hit him with the back of my hand, and I think there is no question but that the Lord led me to do it. If I had slapped him with my open palm, it would have been an insult because that is the way one treats a baby. They would have killed me instantly. If I had struck him with my fist, those men would have put so many spears in me that I would have looked like a pincushion.

But a chief rebukes a brave warrior by slapping him across the chest with the back of his hand! I had never heard of such a thing, but the fact that I did this, plus the fact that I stood straight and tall, plus the fact that I, instinctively, held the chief by the wrist to prevent him from leaving…all of this convinced him that I was a great chief and a mighty warrior! (Actually, in all the history of the world, there has never been a preacher as scared as I was at that minute!)

The second smart thing I did was to yell for help at the top of my voice! "*Bwana* Paul—heyyyyyy—*Bwana* Paul," I hollered… and hollered and hollered! Finally Mr. Paul, sitting outside the camp, heard me and dashed up through the trees until he could see what was going on. He immediately recognized the Lotukas and ran back to get one of our men to act as an interpreter. Unfortunately, however, our four boys had also seen the Lotukas and had high-tailed it for the tall timber! Honestly—Mr. Paul had to chase down one of our fellows and drag him to a meeting with the spearmen.

Don't Insult a Texan!

When they arrived I was still holding the chief by the wrist. He had made no resistance and the other men were still standing just about where they had been when I clobbered their friend with his own spear.

In *Bangala*, *Bwana* Paul asked our native to ask the Lotuka chief why they had tried to kill me.

"We don't like Englishmen," the chief said.

"Englishmen!" I yelled, "I'm not English, you knothead, I'm a Texan!"

And with that I whopped him again across the chest with the back of my hand!

...After awhile things got calmed down. The chief was sorry he had not known we were friends and we shook hands all around.

Wrestling

When the excitement had died down, I went back around behind a large tree and earnestly thanked God that my life had been spared. I also vomited and retched again and again.

The warriors became very friendly. I loaded my cameras with fresh film and took pictures of them throwing spears at an imaginary lion. Then they put on a wrestling exhibition for us. The largest fellow in the group walked up to me with a grin and asked if I would like to wrestle with him. My heart skipped about forty beats as I looked at the big fellow. He had more muscles than Tarzan! I finally explained that this chief didn't wrestle with ordinary warriors!

Most of the time they wrestled I was sitting on the ground, leaning back against the tree. I was running a fever and had a splitting headache. And most of the time the poor fellow I had socked with the spear sat beside me. Doubtless he had a splitting headache, too. His nose was so swollen that his eyes were almost closed and a big ridge ran from his nose to the top of his forehead. He seemed to like me, though, and both *Bwana* Paul and I had the impression that he was rather proud of the fact that he had been laid low by so mighty a chief!

The eight Lotukas stayed with us all day long. Or I should say, they stayed with *me* all day long. If I sat down, they sat down in a circle around me. If I stood up, they stood up. If I moved, they followed at my heels.

We tried to talk to them about the Lord, but our one native who could speak their language did so very poorly. The language barrier plus their ignorance of the Gospel made the difficulties insurmountable.

When twilight came they reluctantly left. We were not sorry to see them go, but we were sorry we never saw them again.

Practical Praying

A year later Austin Paul and I met in Philadelphia where I was conducting a revival campaign. One evening he told about the incident. After the service a sissy young man came to the platform and piously said, "Brother Rice, I certainly am surprised at your behavior. The idea of you striking that poor heathen. If you had been a real man of God, you would have prayed."

"But I did pray," I replied, "and my prayer was scriptural, practical, and to the point. When I swung that spear I said, 'Lord, don't let me miss this fellow!'"

Am I joking when I say that I prayed? No, I'm not! I did pray and God did answer my prayer. I wasn't trying to kill the fellow or even seriously injure him. I was trying to keep him from killing me. I prayed and then did the best I knew to do. And everyone who went through the terrible blood bath a few months later still marvels that one lone, sick preacher struck a warrior with his own spear, slapped the chief, and bluffed eight Lotukas and got away with it.

The fact is, I prayed and did my best. I honestly believe God answered my prayer. I certainly had never thought of having such an experience. And when it happened I dead sure had no time to think what I should do. Yet, we now know I did about the only thing I could have done. It's a wonder I didn't run but if I had, I probably wouldn't have lasted ten seconds.

"Give Us..."

There is an old saying that "God helps those who help themselves." Perhaps it would be more true that God helps those who ask for His guidance and then follow it. Jesus said, *"Ask, and it shall be given you; seek, and ye shall find; knock, and it shall be opened unto you"—Matthew 7:7.*

Jesus said we are to ask, look, and knock.

If I needed a job, I would certainly pray. But I wouldn't just sit around in my room waiting for a job to find me. I would try to find someone who needed a helper and then I would knock on his door.

David felt Goliath should be put out of the way. I am sure he prayed about it. He also put a stone in his sling. Did the stone or the prayer kill the giant? It was both. David was willing to do what he could and he prayed it would be enough.

Jesus said we are to pray for daily bread. Does this mean we can loaf around and when it is mealtime we can pray and God will drop bread on the table? Of course not. We are to pray that God will bless our efforts to earn our bread.

I realize there are times when we pray and there is not one thing in the world we can do ourselves. But there are many times when the dear Lord would lead us to the answer to our prayers if only we would follow His clear leading.

Winning the Lost

In revivals many people ask us to pray with them for their unsaved loved ones. Yet, so often these same people have never made any attempt to actually win their loved ones. Fathers ask prayer for their sons, yet they do not read the Bible in the home, do not pray, do not see to it that the son is in church, do not talk to the boy about his soul's salvation.

Hundreds—perhaps thousands—of wives ask prayer for their husbands. Yet, upon questioning, I find they have never one time talked to the husband about his need of Christ.

But, Good Neighbor, folks are saved through the Bible. And God has no way of presenting the Gospel of Christ except through *people*—people like you and me. God has always used people to win souls to Christ.

Someone has said we should pray as though everything depended upon God and work as though everything depended upon us.

If you have unsaved loved ones, earnestly ask God for their salvation. Ask God what you can do to help win them. Perhaps you are the very one God will use to explain the plan of salvation and bring them to a decision. Or perhaps God will lead you to arrange a meeting between the unsaved one and a pastor or evangelist or some other Christian who can lead him to Christ. Or perhaps you can get your unsaved one to go to church to hear an evangelistic sermon that will bring him to Christ. Or perhaps God will lead you to just the right book or tract that will help.

7

BEWARE THE BUFFALO

The great buffalo of Africa needs a press agent. When one thinks of the Dark Continent he is likely to think of lions and leopards and elephants. But who ever thinks of buffalo?

And yet Selouis, one of Africa's Great White Hunters, ranks the buffalo as the most dangerous animal in all Africa. And I never met a missionary who did much hunting who did not have a great respect for the vicious prowess of the buffalo.

In the first place, the African buffalo is just plain big. In an ordinary herd there will be many that will weigh more than two thousand pounds. He is not only large but is endowed with those characteristics that would make any vicious animal a killer.

Being a thick-skinned animal, he is tough and hard to stop, and harder to kill. A number of missionaries told me that thick-skinned animals were hard to kill, while thin-skinned animals were comparatively easy to kill. Even a lion, king of the beasts, will eventually die if solidly hit anyplace in his body by a bullet. I do not know about that; but I do know, from personal experience, that a big buffalo is mighty hard to stop unless shot through the brain or through the heart.

Then, too, a buffalo has unusually sharp eyesight, a keen sense of smell, and acute hearing. Add to this a good intellect and an ornery disposition and you've got more trouble in a minute than you can handle in a month of Sundays!

Elephants are big and strong and tough and are sometimes enraged by the very scent of man. But an elephant does not have keen eyesight and must rely largely upon his nose and ears. They have been known to pass within a few feet of a man without seeing him.

The rhinoceros is big and strong and tough and angry. But he not only has weak eyes but a weak mind. If he charges a man and misses, he may abruptly stop and begin grazing, having forgotten all about the fact that he has just made a furious charge.

But Mr. Buffalo is of a different breed. I remember Austin Paul introducing me to one native who had great white scars on his legs and ankles. He had been charged by a buffalo and had climbed up in a small tree. The buffalo, however, by standing on its hind legs could reach the man with its teeth! It had tried again and again to pull the man down from the tree as the long scars on the fellow's legs testified.

Wounded Animals Remember

Actually, there usually is not as much danger from wild animals as one might think. As a rule, lions or leopards, elephants or buffalo will avoid or even run from men when given the chance. An elephant, for example, is not likely to charge a man unless he has previously been wounded by some hunter. But if an elephant has been badly hurt, whether by a bullet or a spear, and has lived through it—look out! When he smells man, he may go into a trumpeting rage and destroy anything from an automobile to a village in an effort to kill. This is one reason a hunter should always find and kill a wounded animal. He should also do it for numerous reasons, of course. Sometimes a leopard or a lion will devour an African child that has wandered away from his mother. Having once tasted the flesh of a human, these animals sometimes stalk natives until they are trapped and killed.

Incidentally, when a hunter is charged by some large animal and is able to wound it—he never knows if the shock and pain will discourage the animal so that it will run away or if it will so enrage the beast that it will fight to the death.

On Safari

Missionaries Austin Paul and Harold Amstutz and Harold's teenage son, David, some natives, and I were on a combination hunting and preaching mission. We reckoned on being gone from Amstutz' village for five or six days. We drove the old Pie-wagon until we came to a stream it could not cross. We traveled on that day without incident. But on the second day two things happened that I will never forget.

First, we met a man and his family on the trail. Two young wives were carrying a twelve-year-old girl in a sling. They had a pole which they carried on their shoulders and the sling, made of dirty canvas, was suspended from this pole. The girl was delirious. With our bodies we shaded her, and Austin Paul felt her forehead. "This girl is burning up with fever," he exclaimed. I put my hand on her forehead and, sure enough, she was suffering a high fever.

We gave her water and aspirin and they went on their way. They were going, they said, to the white missionary doctor.

That was all there was to that incident, but three days later two native runners chased us down to inform us that the girl had died and that the disease had been a highly contagious one. The medical missionary thought we ought to know! Austin Paul and I had touched the girl and the others in the group had stood near her.

What to do? We talked it over and decided to go on. After all, if we were going to catch the disease, it would strike before we could get back to our headquarters anyway. If we had not contracted the disease, it would only be a waste of our time to go back. So we decided to go on. But for the next several days, I kept wondering what the first symptoms of the disease would be! And, if worse came to worse, I wondered what the others would do with our bodies!

The other memorable thing was my encounter with the buffalo. We were out of meat and had made our way to the top of a small mountain to survey the countryside. Suddenly, far down the mountain and to our left, we saw a deer walking along a game trail. If one of us hurried straight down, we would be in the game trail in time to intercept the deer, and I volunteered for the job.

Down the side of the little mountain I went as fast as I could go. At last, huffing and puffing and sweating, I descended to a game trail that I presumed to be the one we had seen from far above. Right in front of me the trail made a bend, and foliage on each side of it was so dense that an animal would not see me before he was almost upon me. An ideal spot. So, I didn't even hide in the brush but stood right in the middle of the trail, gun cocked, and my finger on the trigger.

I could hear the big bushbuck coming. In another moment we would be face to face. What a cinch! Suddenly, I heard him break into a run. Evidently something had startled him but, I grinned to myself, he was going to be a lot more startled when he came around that bend in the trail. There would be meat around the campfire tonight!

But it turned out that I was the startled one. When that big bushbuck came running around the curve of the trail—it wasn't a bushbuck but a giant bull buffalo! This Great White Hunter, landing on the wrong trail, had been scented by the buffalo and had become the hunted one!

I fired the powerful Magnum rifle and heard the *thud* of the bullet hitting solid.

> The buffalo bellered and ran at me,
> I hollered, too, and ran for a tree!

(Great guns—poetry at a time like this!)

I didn't have time to climb a tree, but I figured I could run around and around that tree faster than the buffalo could. Moreover, I intended to keep shootin' at him while I ran. But the buffalo did not chase me. Instead, he thundered on down the trail and disappeared from sight.

The rest of the party came down the mountain to join me and I told them what had happened. We walked only a few feet to find a heavy blood spoor. Obviously, I had hit him solidly and it would just be a matter of time until the big beast would drop. We followed the blood spoor until the buffalo left the trail and went into a finger of the jungle.

At the edge of the jungle Austin Paul stopped.

"We'd better let a couple of natives track him into the jungle," *Bwana* Paul said, "while we wait here."

"Nothing doing," I remonstrated, "I shot that buffalo and I intend to go in and finish him."

Bwana Paul told me that white men were killed every year doing that very thing. "That big brute is smart," *Bwana* Paul said, "and he knows that you are going to follow him into the jungle.

He will hide and wait; and if he has any strength at all, he will kill you before he dies."

So two African natives went into the jungle while we waited. It must have been an hour or more later that they came back out and told Mr. Paul and Mr. Amstutz what they had found. But they told it in the native language and I could not understand it. When they were finished, Austin Paul turned to me and grinned as he said, "All right, now you follow that blood spoor and get your buffalo. I'm not going to tell you what these men said except that they did find the buffalo and he is waiting for you in the jungle."

So we went in, with me leading the way. The trail of blood was so heavy that the most amateurish hunter could have followed the spoor. But one thing kept running through my mind—I simply must see the big beast before it saw me. I held my gun, safety off, up in firing position, and made my way, foot by foot, along the buffalo's trail.

Again and again, I stopped to peer ahead through the gloom. In some places the overhead foliage was so thick it was difficult to see more than a few yards ahead.

Suddenly Austin Paul screamed, "There he is!" and I just about jumped out of my skin. Sure enough, there the buffalo was just a few feet in front of me. It was lying dead in the trail.

Bwana Paul and *Bwana* Amstutz had known all along, of course, that the animal was dead. The natives had told them so. But they had really enjoyed watching me creep so carefully along that trail, and now they hollered in delight at Mr. Paul's joke!

All of us were aware of the fact, however, that had the beast still been alive—Rice would have been planted that day in that jungle.

In my anxiety to see the buffalo while he was still far enough ahead that I would have plenty of time to aim and fire, I had overlooked the fact that a fellow simply cannot see that far ahead in the jungle. As a result, I had walked right up on the great beast without even seeing him until Austin Paul's yell had scared the living daylights out of me!

The massive horns were hacked off the huge head and were later shipped to me. I had them mounted and today they hang in the living room of my home on the Bill Rice Ranch.

Never Count on Seeing the Buffalo First!

Many times I have remembered that experience. I thought sure I would see the buffalo before he saw me; that I would have plenty of time to prepare to take care of myself after I saw him. But it wouldn't have worked out that way had the buffalo still been alive.

I realize now how presumptuous it was of me, a greenhorn, to think that I would see the buffalo before he saw me. He knew exactly the trail I would follow. He would hear me when I was yet hundreds of feet away. His sense of smell could tell him if I were perspiring from running or if I had been slowly stalking him. And his sense of smell could also tell him if I were frightened or nervous or calm. What's more, was at home in the jungle and his eyes were accustomed to the gloom. I was a stranger.

I often marvel that I could have been so foolish. But I certainly learned a lesson: Never count on seeing the buffalo first! I should have expected to meet him at every step of the way.

How Far Up the Trail?

In Luke 12:16-21 we find the story Jesus told of the rich fool. This man was a farmer. He had been an unusually successful one, too. Evidently he had both studied and worked hard to be a good farmer. And it had paid off—it had made him rich.

As he had walked down the path of life, he had planned what he would do in the days ahead. He would tear down his barns and build greater ones. He would enjoy life. He would eat, drink, and be merry.

Oddly enough, however, he did not make any plans about meeting death in the trail ahead. It wasn't that he did not know he must meet death sooner or later. He knew that, but he gave it little consideration. He thought it would be "later" rather than "sooner" that he met death.

But to his dismay, even as he made his plans, death was just a step ahead in the trail!

"Thou fool," God said unto him, ***"this night thy soul shall be required of thee!"*** So this successful man had not really been a wise man after all. He was a fool. The buffalo saw him first.

Death on the Trail Ahead

Good Neighbor, any man is foolish who does not face the fact that death awaits each one of us on the trail ahead. How far ahead death may be we do not know. But we do know that ***"... it is appointed unto men once to die, but after this the judgment"***— *Hebrews 9:27.*

I have talked with many a man about his soul who has said, "I'll worry about getting saved when the time comes." But the man who thinks he will wait until he faces death to do something about his salvation will probably find that he comes upon death unexpectedly and that there is no time for preparation.

Hebrews 2:3 says, ***"How shall we escape, if we neglect so great salvation;...."***

Good Neighbor, it is dangerous, it is foolish, and it is wicked to walk the trail of life unprepared when you could be saved this very minute. With all the sincerity of my heart, I urge you to turn to the Lord Jesus Christ. Receive Him as your Lord and your Saviour. And do it right now.

8

THE LEOPARD DANCE

The Nile River, seen from the air as it flows through the Sudan, can be a thrilling but awesome sight. I have seen giant crocodiles sunning themselves side by side in long rows on its banks. Elephants and many other beasts of the African bush may be seen by the hundreds along its shores.

But the times we crossed, Pie-wagon and all, on the ferries it seemed no different than any large, muddy American river.

And yet, there is a romance to the Nile that may not be found in any other river on earth. I have traveled almost its entire length, flying its winding course through deserts, sailing on its waters in Egypt; and I never see its waters without thinking of Cleopatra, of the Pharaohs, of Moses—of history!

The days we had to spend in the Sudan were all too few and we prayed that God would help us make the most of them. And the Lord surely answered our prayer. Besides revival services we made a safari into the bush to explore the possibilities of a new mission station where we met the Lotukas, preached Christ in a number of scattered villages, and conducted a Bible conference with Sudan missionaries who had gathered together for the purpose.

Scorpions

Everywhere I went in Africa the natives seemed to love and admire the missionaries. And because the missionaries were always kind and gracious to me, the natives were, too. Any time I needed a guide or helper I could count on about 'stenn dozen volunteers. The overall friendliness and kindness of both missionaries and natives completely won my heart, and I will always have a real love for Africa and its peoples. Their willingness to do me a favor just about backfired when Austin Paul told one of the natives I wanted to see a scorpion.

One morning *Bwana* Paul came to my room just as I had finished dressing. Just as he came in, I reached for one of my boots and pulled it on. "In this area," Mr. Paul said, "it is never wise to pull on a boot until you first turn it upside down and shake it. A scorpion may be hiding in it and his poison can make a man desperately sick for several days or even kill him."

I had never seen a scorpion and he explained that they looked for all the world like a midget lobster with two big claws, several legs to run on, and a jointed tail. The scorpion, however, was only two or three inches long. It attacks by seizing its victim with its powerful front claws and then curling its tail over its own head and "stinging" its prey. I told *Bwana* Paul I would like to take a picture of one and he said he would ask one of the natives to get one for me.

About an hour later a young fellow came up with a large covered tin can. *Bwana* Paul yelled that he was the fellow who had the scorpion for me, and the fellow and I walked out to a large flat rock. I set up my camera and tripod and this fellow turned the can upside down on the rock and slipped the lid out from under it. I had just supposed that he had found a scorpion and had killed it and it struck me as rather unusual that he would take such precautions with a dead scorpion. Nevertheless, I aimed the camera, pushed the button to start the motor, and motioned for him to raise the tin can.

The young man gave me a puzzled look and just stood there with his hand holding the tin can down against the flat rock. But the camera was running and film was precious, so I reached over and put my hand on his and said, "Okay, let's pick the tin can up and see it."

He still just stood there, so I just put my hand over his and raised the can up so I could see the dead scorpion.

Dead scorpion, my hind leg! There must have been fifty or sixty of the critters in that big can and the moment I lifted it they began scattering with their venomous little tails curled over their heads, in every direction! The barefooted native yelled and ran! I yelled and ran past him!

Excitement in the Village

One morning a slender young missionary named William Beatty told me he had to deliver a native to a village some twelve or fifteen miles away. The fellow had been injured and had been brought to the clinic, but now he was being released. They felt the long walk home would be too much for him so Mr. Beatty was going to take him in his pickup. He asked me to go along for the ride and said we could probably stop for a service or so in villages going and coming.

We delivered the sick man and were driving down a well-traveled trail that would, we knew, eventually lead to a village. Young Beatty and I were riding in the cab of the pickup and three black men from the mission station were standing up in the bed of the truck.

Presently, in the distance we saw a small village of grass houses. We guessed, from the number of houses, that probably about one hundred people lived in the little village. And we saw something else—it looked like the entire population was chasing itself around and around, helter-skelter among the houses without any apparent motive, method, or pattern!

As we drew nearer, we could hear men and women yelling and screaming and singing at the top of their voices. I supposed at first they were having an old-fashioned, knock-down-drag-'em-out-free-for-all brawl, but as we drew nearer we saw that no one was fighting. They were just singing and dancing and having a grand old time!

It seemed unbelievable to me then and seems incredible as I tell it now, but we drove that pickup truck into the edge of that crowd so that they actually had to detour around us as they ran and danced—and it was still three or four minutes before a single one of them realized we were there! It was almost as though they were in some kind of hypnotic trance—as though they were mesmerized.

I jumped out of the cab with my movie camera, climbed over the rack into the bed of the pickup, adjusted the camera, and had begun taking moving pictures before we were noticed! But when they did notice us, business sure did pick up. A bunch of them, both men and women, ran to the rear of our truck, grabbed one of our natives, threw him on the ground, and began stomping on him.

Like a Leopard

I yelled at *Bwana* Beatty, "Stay in the cab and lock the doors," and jumped off the back of the truck into the middle of the squirming, wriggling, howling bunch that was stomping our man. Grabbing naked arms, necks, and shoulders, I began yanking the villagers off the prostrate native while yelling at the top of my voice, "Cut it out! Leave him alone! We're friends" and, "*te, te, te!* (No, no, no)." I had yelled at William to stay in the cab and lock the doors, but he didn't mind worth a nickel. He came running around the pickup, pushing his way through the villagers until he reached me. In native dialect he yelled that we were friends and that we had come with good news and that I had something important to say to them.

Actually, the most important thing I could think of to say was, "Good-by!" We finally managed to shove everyone away and helped our friend to his feet. He wasn't badly hurt but he was badly shaken and he was badly scared. As soon as he could get up he scrambled back into the bed of the pickup with our other two natives who had neither made an effort to escape nor to help us.

When things had quieted down somewhat, two men wearing leopard skins hanging down their backs came to talk with us. It was the chief and his eldest son. They were having a leopard dance, he explained, to celebrate a wonderful event. And it really had been quite a wonderful event, at that.

The night before, two leopards had entered the grass hut of one of the villagers. A goat had been tied at the corner of this man's hut. (Often a native will keep a goat tied in or near his hut to appease any bloodthirsty lion or leopards that might invade the village.) But two grown leopards had entered the hut and awakened him. Thinking there was only one leopard in the hut with him, the poor man was still so frightened he became hysterical. No man is a match for a leopard, but he grabbed a machete and began slashing wildly into the darkness, screaming at the top of his voice all the while. Of course, the entire village was awakened; and when they ran with torches to his hut, they found him on his knees flailing away with that machete at *two* dying leopards!

It is absolutely incredible that one man alone could kill two leopards in the pitch darkness of the small hut. Equally incredible was the fact that the warrior not only came out of the battle alive but completely unscathed! He hadn't even been scratched.

The villagers had quickly made a fire and skinned the two leopards, and the men and boys had then completely devoured both beasts, eating the flesh raw! This they had done so that they would be as strong and cunning as their enemy, the leopard!

After all that excitement no one, of course, wanted to go back to sleep. So they had begun dancing to celebrate their victory over the leopards. The chief and his oldest son claimed the still-bloody hides as their own and had tied them to their backs.

Except for a few pauses for beer or rest, the villagers had danced and shouted and sung the rest of the night and were still at it at mid-morning when we drove up.

Brotherhood of the Leopards

We tried to get them calmed down enough so that we could tell them of Jesus Christ. But this was one congregation we couldn't have held with a rope! A few minutes after we had begun speaking, the entire crowd took off again on a dead run, circling around and around the houses. They were celebrating the fact, they said, that they were now brothers of the leopard.

We stayed for perhaps half an hour longer. During this time I took moving pictures of the leopard dance and then we departed.

How strange, I thought, that they wanted to be brothers with the leopard. The powerful, cunning, sly, thieving leopard is doubtless the most-feared beast in Africa. And yet, many African natives longed to be like the leopard.

In fact, there was a secret society of natives who wore leopard skins, leopard masks, and tortured and killed their victims with leopard claws. In one of our meetings a man who had belonged to that group was converted and presented me with a small ivory statue of a "leopardman."

These men, by eating the raw flesh of the leopard, hoped to become like the leopards. How strange that they would be drawn to the very beast that would devour their children, kill their wives, and maim their own bodies. And yet, perhaps, this is a trait characteristic of carnal human beings. Any man who can read the Bible, read history, read daily newspapers, or just look around him, can see what destruction is wrought by sin and by Satan on every hand. Surely Satan has brought death and destruction to the children of men. And yet, around the world, there are men and women whose chief aim in life is to become more steeped in sin, to become more like Satan!

9

BABOON BY A LONG SHOT

"Dear Princess:
"This is going to be a typical missionary letter—I am sick!"

This is the way I began the letter I wrote my lovely wife during the revival campaign at Aba. Actually, I became sick five days after arriving in the Congo. It has always seemed strange to me, because I had been unusually healthy all of my life. I hardly know what it is, even today, to have a headache or a bad cold. I have traveled around the world and have eaten native food in every foreign country I have visited, with no ill effects. But in Africa it was different.

My first engagement in Africa was to preach at the bi-annual missionary conference at Rethy. Missionaries had gathered from many places and I was to be the key speaker. But I missed the first two days. I had all the symptoms of malaria, but the young British doctor who examined me said it could not be malaria because I had not been in Africa long enough. No one, he said, could get malaria in just five days.

He gave me sulfa in large quantities and other antibiotics, and after the first two days I was able to speak twice daily at the conference.

For the next three months, I suffered often from diarrhea and always from nausea. The worst thing, though, was the mysterious swelling of my hands and feet. Suddenly the heel or ball of a foot would become red, swollen, and sore, as though it had been seriously bruised. Usually, within a day's time, it would return to normal and then a day or so later, the heel of a hand or my wrist would go through the same thing.

During the months I was in Africa, however, I missed only one revival service because of illness (it was in the afternoon) and the first two conference days at Rethy.

Finally, we were in Oicha for a revival and Dr. Becker took a blood sample. He found that malaria was so thick in my blood stream that one faction was yelling to the other, "Yankee, go home!" He gave me some stuff that greatly relieved me. However, I suffered from malaria for a number of years after returning home, and I still have an occasional recurrence of the swelling of a hand or foot.

Baboons in the Garden

Anyway, it was at Aba that I missed the one revival service that I mentioned above. I had preached in the morning and God had given a wonderful service. When we finally got away to go to our headquarters for lunch, I made the mistake of pulling my boots off. When it was time to go back for the afternoon service, my feet were so swollen I simply could not get the boots back on again. I pulled and heaved and sweated—but without success. So I stayed in the house while the others went to the revival service. The Amstutz' splendid teenage son, David, stayed with me.

We were talking when one of the natives who tended their garden came running into the room. He was excited about something and he explained the matter to David in native dialect. It seemed that a tribe of baboons had been into the garden again and they had driven them off. But the baboons were still nearby and would not leave. One of them—probably a scout—could be seen in the top of a giant tree on the side of the mountain.

David ran outside with the native and presently came back and told me that, sure enough, upon the side of the mountain a large baboon was keeping watch from the top of a large dead tree. He was waiting for the excitement to die down so that the tribe could return to the garden.

The Long Shot

Baboons are a real headache to missionaries and natives alike. They live in tribes and they seem to organize their plans similar to the organization of a flock of crows. They post lookouts and if one is attacked, the entire tribe may rush to his defense. Even leopards, vicious fighters though they are, seldom tackle a grown baboon. The baboon is not only a fierce fighter but all of his brothers and uncles and cousins will probably rush in to help him out. Sometimes a leopard will seize an unwary baby baboon, run off with it, and then play with it like a cat with a mouse before devouring it.

(Incidentally, one can usually tell when baboons are nearby because of the pungent odor of their urine. On a jungle trail one day I stopped, sniffed the air, and said, "Hey, somebody has been spilling iodine around here." My companions promptly had hysterics! It was the funniest thing they ever heard—a real knee-popper!

They told me what it was and, sure enough, a bit later we came upon the tribe of baboons.)

When David came back to tell me about the baboon in the large dead tree upon the mountainside, he asked if I thought I could hit it with his .22 Hornet. I walked outside in my sock feet to take a look.

Standing beneath a tree to shade their eyes, the native gardeners were talking and pointing. I walked up and I couldn't even see the tree they were talking about. David put his rifle on a limb and pointed it, and I looked down the barrel until I saw the tree to which he was referring. We were standing on the edge of a mountain and across the valley and far up the side of the next mountain there was a large dead tree. I looked and I looked, but I couldn't see any baboon. I took David's rifle and, by looking through the telescopic sight, examined the tree limb by limb. Finally, I spotted the beast. He was facing us in a picture-book stance, in a fork near the top of the tree. He was standing with his arms and legs spread wide, holding the branches on either side. He was so far away that even through the scope he looked hardly larger than a squirrel.

"That fellow is a long way off," I said to Dave. "Do you believe this Hornet will reach that far?"

Dave said that he thought it would since it had one of the longest ranges of any rifle in the world. I knew that if I did hit that overgrown monkey it would be the longest shot I had ever made in my life. Frankly, it would be just luck if I hit him—but I have always been a lucky shot.

I found a sturdy branch that was just about the right height for me to lay the rifle across to steady it. It just happened that, two feet away, there was another branch about the same height and I rested the end of the rifle barrel on it. Then—and I suppose this would not happen again in a million years—I discovered an amazing coincidence. On the limb nearest me there was a large knot just to the right of the gun barrel. On the other limb there was a small fork just to the left of the end of the barrel. By pushing the butt of the gun to the right and the front of the barrel to the left, the rifle was held almost rock steady...and when I looked through the telescopic sight the hairs crossed right square dab on that baboon's chest! I pulled down on the butt of the gun just a hair so the crosshairs of the scope were on the creature's chest at the base of his neck. (The bullet would drop some at that distance.)

Then I pulled the trigger.

The recoil of the rifle knocked it off target for a moment, but when I sighted again at the tree—the baboon was gone. The natives were yelling and David said, "You hit him, you hit him!"

"How do you know I hit him?" I asked. "How do you know he didn't just jump down?"

"Because," David explained, "these natives say the baboon went over backwards and fell head first."

How in the world those fellows could even see that creature so far away, I don't know. But they were sure that the baboon had been killed and two of them began running down the side of the mountain to go after it.

Right on the Flea

About that time *Bwana* Paul returned from the afternoon service and David explained to him what had happened. We stood and watched the two natives go down the side of our mountain, across the valley, and start up the neighboring mountain. Finally, they reached the base of the big dead tree. We saw them pick up something and we could hear them yelling, but we could not understand their words.

"Great guns," I said, "I actually did hit him!"

"Oh, Great White Hunter," Austin Paul said as he bowed and scraped, "please tell this unworthy person where thou didst smite yon beast."

"I'll be glad to, *Sahib*," I grandly replied. "I'm always glad to help thou fellers if it costs me nothing. I struck yon thieving brute where a flea was resting in the center of his chest, three inches below his neck."

Again and again, *Bwana* Paul yelled to the two men who were bringing back the baboon, "Where was he hit? Where was he hit?" Finally, the men came close enough that they could understand and they yelled back in reply, "In the mouth!"

"Maybe," I said, "that critter noticed the flea and bent his head down to bite it just as I pulled the trigger. That's how come he got smote in his kisser instead of his chest."

When they brought the baboon to us, however, we discovered an amazing thing; although the critter had a little blood on his mouth, the bullet had struck barely to the right of the center of his chest—three inches below the place where his neck joined his body!

Shaking his head in amazement, Austin Paul said this was a record of some kind and he was going to measure the distance. So he walked down the side of the mountain, across the valley, and up the other side to the great tree, carefully counting his steps. Later, he sat down with pencil and paper and figured that, straight across, the distance had been approximately five hundred yards—almost one-third of a mile!

My reputation as a crack marksman was made. I modestly declared that it had been just a lucky shot, but they didn't believe me. Just a couple of days before, I had knocked down a running deer with a six-shooter (pure blind luck!); and now I had not only hit the baboon at an incredible distance, but had told exactly where I had hit him!

Although I was very modest about the whole thing, I never did get around to telling anyone—until now—about that knot and fork on the two branches that had held that rifle as though in a vise!

Long Shots Are Better Than No Shots

Since my boyhood days, hunting has been a way of life for me. I rarely ever shoot any living creature unless I need it for food or unless it is a pest. When I do shoot—I do not like long shots. I would far rather be near enough that there is a possibility of a solid hit.

But many times we have had meat for our campfire because I had taken that one last shot at a rapidly disappearing guinea hen or rabbit or deer. I learned a good many years ago that a fellow has a better chance of hitting something with a long shot than with no shot at all!

And I have learned the same thing in gospel work. I am an evangelist. I have conducted revival campaigns from coast to coast in the States and in many foreign lands. Again and again, I have been in revivals that did not turn out as we had prayed and expected they would. I have been in situations that have been heartbreaking, disappointing, discouraging—seemingly hopeless. And yet only twice in all these years have I ever left a revival campaign. (Both of those times were because of immorality among the revival sponsors.)

I remember a large union campaign when everything seemed to go wrong. In the middle of the series the associate evangelist, song leader, soloist, and I met for our time of daily planning and prayer. These three men announced that they were through. We had been thwarted on every hand. We were having only a few conversions nightly and they were thoroughly disgusted. They were through.

"Fellas," I said after a bit, "I know exactly how you feel. I feel much the same way. We have been doublecrossed and we have fallen among thieves. But we are having a few people saved every night, and I cannot help but believe that it is far better to win a few souls to Christ than to win none at all."

We all stayed and suddenly the power of God was upon the meeting in an unusual way. Great crowds came, scores walked the aisles to accept Christ, and we rejoiced in a great victory.

All meetings have not turned out so happily; but it is still far better to try to win someone, although the possibility of doing so may seem small, than not to try at all.

Harold and Jane Amstutz

Mr. and Mrs. Amstutz at that very station of Aba are a wonderful example of this truth. An outstanding couple in every way, they left a popular and fruitful ministry in America to go to the Dark Continent where everything seemed to go wrong. David, then a little boy, became critically ill. For a while he hovered between life and death. When he finally passed the crisis and was on the way to recovery, some of the other missionaries suggested perhaps they should return to the States. It was feared that David would never fully regain his health if they stayed in Africa.

But the Amstutzes said no, God had led them to Africa and in Africa they would stay.

A short time later Jane, a beautiful and talented woman, was struck by the same disease. She, too, hovered between life and death. When she passed the crisis and was on the way to recovery, it was again suggested that perhaps the Amstutzes should return to the States. Again they refused and stayed by their post.

Then, Harold and Jane went on *safari* into the bush. They had been traveling for three days in an old station wagon when he suffered nausea and a sharp pain in his side. They realized it was an attack of appendicitis. Surely if they stopped and rested, he would be all right. But his condition grew worse. Making a makeshift bed for him in the back of the car, Jane began the long drive back. There was no marked road. She had to rely upon her sense of direction and by-pass the hills, find shallow places in the streams where she could cross, and circle around patches of deep woods when she could.

After three days and nights, with her husband often in delirium always in pain, she arrived at a mission station and "it just happened" that the doctor was there. Although more than certain that peritonitis had already set in, they placed Harold on an old table and the doctor operated on him. It seemed there was almost no hope that he would live.

But live he did! The ordeal had been so severe, however, that his strength returned very slowly. The field council met and said to the Amstutzes, in effect,

"Each of you has undergone a serious illness that may well affect your health for the rest of your life. If you stay here, it may be that you will be so handicapped that you will not be able to have a full and complete ministry. Perhaps you ought to go back to the States."

To this the Amstutzes replied, "Well or sick, God has led us here. And we can certainly do more for the Africans here than we can if we return home. Unless God clearly leads us back to the States, we are going to stay here until He takes us to Heaven."

And stay they did! When I was there some time later, Harold still walked in a slightly stooped position. But he had built a work that was one of the largest and strongest in the entire Congo!

The Amstutzes had taken the long shot—and they thank God they did!

I believe this is what the Lord was trying to get across to us when He caused Paul to write to Timothy, "*...be instant in season, out of season....*" I think He meant that Timothy should preach when he had a good opportunity and he should preach when he had a poor one. He should preach when everything was favorable and he should preach when everything was unfavorable.

The winning of one is far better than the winning of none!

10

THE WILD MAN
OF THE SEMLIKI

In the scheduling of the revival campaigns, Austin Paul had wisely scheduled two brief rest periods. He had known how strenuous the revival campaigns would be. Both of us thought we ought to make the most of the time we had together and so our custom was to schedule five services a day in the revival campaigns. As a rule Austin Paul, one other man (sometimes a native pastor, at times the local missionary), and I would speak in the three morning services. An invitation would be given following my message. Those who came forward were carefully dealt with and this usually took from one to two hours. Then, as a rule, we had one major service in the afternoon with me preaching and giving an invitation. Again we would deal with the people who came forward. Then we had the evening service at dark, with me preaching and giving an invitation. Dealing with those who came forward could again take from one to two hours. The attendance for these three major services often averaged more than five thousand people per service! Besides these we often had brief revival services In small villages, in market places, and along the roadside!

As I look back, I wonder how in the world we found the physical strength to do it. And, remember, *Bwana* Paul had suffered a cancer operation just two years before! He was twenty years older than I, but he hadn't stopped to look at a calendar for so long that he didn't realize it!

But we were both glad to have those two brief times to rest and relax, eat and sleep, pray and study, and take life easy.

On the Semliki

We drove the Pie-wagon and a pickup truck down to the Semliki Valley, *Bwana* Paul had chosen this location because it was isolated and because there was so much game we would not have to walk far to get meat for our meals. Besides, lions inhabit the place and one just might wander into our camp.

As we drove into camp that first day we spooked a small *bodi* (it is called a small deer although it looks more like an antelope to me). We stopped the car and I stepped out and shot it.

That night we cut steaks off the deer and then hung the remainder of the carcass up in a tree just a few feet from the tarpaulin which we had stretched between trees as a shade by day and a shelter by night. The next morning, the deer was gone. None of us had heard a thing, but tracks beneath the tree told the story. A large lion had come into our camp and had walked off with our breakfast! This gave us an idea, and that day we killed a big bushbuck and hung it from the same tree. This time, however, we tied the carcass with a big stout rope so that a lion could not simply pick it up and walk off with it. We also cut thorns to make a *boma* (fence) around the sleeping blankets. Then we parked the pickup in such a way that the spotlight, when turned on, would be on the carcass. I put my sleeping blanket in the pickup and announced that I was going to sleep there with my rifle. When I heard the lion tugging at the rope it would surely wake me up. I would switch on the light and—*bang*—I would have a lion skin to take home.

But nothing happened that night. I slept like a baby. When I woke up in the morning and looked—the big carcass was gone! A lion had simply chewed the big rope in two and had again walked off with the entire thing. And I do mean he had *walked* off with it. He did not drag it although it had weighed well over a hundred pounds!

That day we killed another big bushbuck and hung it in the same tree. This time we fastened it to the tree with chains. This would fix that nosy lion. The rattling of chains was bound to awaken some of us. But it didn't. I still cannot understand it but the next morning there was just a tiny portion of the deer left hanging onto those chains! Again a lion had walked in and helped himself, and none of us had heard a thing.

Elephants

We were camped in a lovely valley by the river. Actually, to call the Semliki a river at that time of year is bragging on it. It had almost dried up and was just a boggy, swampy, muddy wash with small pools of stagnant water sprinkled everywhere and a few tiny streams trickling down through the riverbed. Wild animals came, every morning and every night, to drink. Elephants trumpeted and wallowed in the mud every evening. Their urine and excrement so fouled the muddy water that we could hardly drink it. Of course, we always boiled our water anyway but this stuff was horrible.

One day we had walked across the marshy, slimy, boggy riverbed to hunt on the other side. After a couple of hours I decided to return to camp. Going over we had made our way across the bog by stepping on tufts of coarse *matete* grass. Even then, we waded knee-deep in some places. On the way back the water was so muddy that there was no way of telling how deep it was and I stepped into a hole up to my armpits. As I turned to climb out, my right boot stuck in the mud and my foot came out of it. I began feeling around with my foot, trying to locate that boot again and couldn't find it. I stood there in that filthy stinking mess working my foot all around and couldn't feel that boot to save my life. Finally, I dove under the water and felt around with my hands until I found it! When I came back to the surface, holding my boot in my hand, I was a mess. My rifle and six-shooter had both been fouled, of course. I struggled on across the swamp, sat down on the far side, and finally managed to get the wet boot back on my foot.

When I walked back into camp I was a sight to behold. I was wet and muddy and smelled like an outhouse. I plopped down on the ground and asked one of the natives to bring me some *my phew*, some hot (boiled) water. Instead of water, he handed me what I took to be a cup of very strong coffee. I took one look at it and said to *Bwana* Paul, "He didn't understand me. I want *my phew*, not coffee." *Bwana* Paul grinned and said, "That is *my phew*—there's no coffee in it."

I tasted it—and promptly threw up! It was too phew-y! "Put some coffee in it," I said, "and I'll try it again."

After I had rested a bit, I took off the filthy clothes I had been wearing and a couple of our natives poured buckets of water over me. It was the filthy water from the river, but at least it got rid of the mud and slime.

I had just started to dress when, for the first time, a small herd of elephants walked toward our camp and then stopped about three hundred yards away. We often saw elephants in the distance but this was the first time any had dared come this close. As we watched, a great big nosy bull left the herd and began walking toward us. Austin, Claudon, and I jumped for our rifles and I, dressed only in a pair of green shorts, jumped into the bed of the pickup. The big bull continued to walk toward us. "If he passes that little bush," Claudon said, "let's fire into the air. If he doesn't turn tail and run he will attack. If we can't stop him we are in real trouble, so shoot to kill."

I steadied the barrel of my rifle across the truck rack and watched the approaching elephant down the sites of my rifle. I hoped the ole jumbo would pass the designated bush. At the moment I was mad at every elephant on earth and especially those that had been using the Semliki as a bathroom. I wondered bitterly why I had ever given a pachyderm a peanut! If that big idiot passed that bush I was going to knock him down with my rifle—and then pour a cup of that water down him to polish him off!

The great beast walked up to the bush and stopped as though he had read our minds. He stood there eyeing us for two or three minutes and then abruptly turned and joined his companions who were now making their way down to the river.

We put our guns down. "I sure would hate to have a giant like that walk in on me unexpectedly," Claudon said. "He didn't mean any harm," *Bwana* Paul grinned, "he just came close enough to get a good look at Bill. That elephant had never seen a Great White Hunter in green shorts before!"

Wild Boar

Early in the morning, Claudon Stauffacher and I walked up the valley to see if we could jump a deer for camp meat. The lions had cleaned us out. Several natives with spears were with us. I suppose we had walked less than a mile when I saw a nice *bodi* several hundred yards ahead. Whispering to the others to wait,

I began creeping up on the animal. Walking in a low crouch, I tried to always keep a tree between me and the deer. One of the natives with a spear was slipping along behind me. In this fashion we had covered more than a hundred yards and I was almost close enough to be sure of a kill.

A moment later, I peered around the trunk of a tree and there was the deer not more than a hundred seventy-five yards away. I had just steadied the rifle barrel against the trunk of a tree when a large wild hog with a string of piglets dashed across the clearing between me and the deer. The deer never did see me, but it was spooked by the big sow and her babies and went bounding off into the trees. Just then a large wild boar made his appearance, following the sow and piglets. I quickly decided that if I couldn't have a deer I would settle for wild boar. I hastily aimed and squeezed the trigger. It was not a good shot.

The boar was angling away from me as he ran and the bullet went through his groin rather than his chest. He ran a few yards and then stopped and sat down. The native behind me yelled and went running out across the clearing toward the boar. He held his spear much as a pole-vaulter holds his pole. It was clear he intended to run the porker through. But the big grunter had other ideas. He stood to his feet and, with his great tusks gleaming, ran at the native. That poor fellow, surprised by the sudden turn of events, threw his spear wildly at the boar—and missed him by a country mile! By the time the native could stop, turn, and get started in the other direction the boar was just a jump behind. I dropped to one knee, aimed the rifle, and squeezed the trigger, knocking the boar dead in his tracks. Actually, I didn't believe the boar could have caught the frightened native, I was worried about another frightened fellow—they were heading back toward me!

The Wild Man

After examining the boar (it was the first one I had seen), I told Claudon I had enough of hunting for the morning and was going back to camp. He and the natives decided to hunt awhile longer.

By this time the sun was hot and I was perspiring freely as I walked back toward camp. After a bit, I came to an unusually large tree and decided it might be nice to rest in the shade for a bit. With my rifle slung over my shoulder, I walked beneath the spreading branches of the great tree intending to sit down against the trunk. Suddenly I looked up—I do not know why—and my heart jumped into my throat. There, high above me and perhaps thirty feet away, I could see through the foliage a large black shape coming toward me, stepping from limb to limb and descending as it came. *It was far too large to be any ape I had seen before—it had to be a gorilla!*

I was scared, but I think I was even more startled and surprised than frightened. Gorillas were supposed to be far away near the Mountains of the Moon. In a split second I had unslung the rifle, worked the bolt, and slammed a powerful Magnum cartridge into the firing chamber. Then, holding the rifle at ready, I slowly began to back up. Quickly I scanned the rest of the great tree, but if there was another creature up there I did not see it. Then the "gorilla" swung down to a large lower limb into plain sight. It wasn't a gorilla at all.

It was a short thick-set man, black as midnight, and naked as the moment he was born!

Thunderstruck with surprise, I looked at the fellow about nine feet above me. I doubt if he was more than five feet tall but he was very broad and thick and powerfully built. His hands and his feet seemed to be unusually large. His head was either shaven or bald. His face was broad with a large flat nose, heavy ridges over his eyes, a large mouth, and thick lips. Staring intently at me, he slowly squatted down on the large limb.

I thought he looked angry so I smiled and greeted him in Bangala, *"Sene Minge!"* There was no change of expression. He just sat up there looking down at me with that piercing stare. In *Kingwana* I tried again, *"Jambo,"* I smiled up at him but still there was no response. Slowly I began backing up again. He arose to a crouch and for a moment I thought he was going to jump down. But he didn't. I continued to back out from under the tree and he just continued to stare without moving again. I backed about fifty feet from the tree and then circled it and continued walking toward our camp, frequently looking back over my shoulder. But I never saw him again.

My two companions, when I told them about it later, said the man obviously was an outcast from his tribe. Probably he had committed some criminal act and had been driven from his village. He would likely spend the rest of his life wandering around, sleeping in hollow trees or caves or whatever shelter could be easily found.

A Real, Honest-to-Goodness Cave Man

I often receive letters from high school and college young people asking me to explain where cave men came from if the Bible story of creation is true.

That poor naked fellow up in that tree is the answer!

There is no denying that there have been men in times past who have lived in caves. In fact, I have been in caves in Texas and in Arizona that were once inhabited by people. And I have seen similar caves in Africa and in Asia. There are also thousands and thousands of people who live in caves right this very moment.

But there never has been a time—in all the history of the world—when men universally lived in caves. All of the pictures you have ever seen and all of the tales you have ever read of brutish creatures—half man and half ape—living in caves, going about naked, and eating their meat raw—all of this is as phony as a three-dollar bill! All of this nonsense is the product of men who are desperately trying to prove an unprovable evolutionary hypothesis.

Cave men have always been the exception rather than the rule. Those whose relics we have discovered were probably either driven off from their fellows because of their behavior or cut off from the others because of accident.

But the history of man does not begin in a cave.

Adam and Eve

Every man and every woman who has ever lived on the face of this earth has been a descendant of Adam and Eve, as we know from Genesis 3:20 and Acts 17:26. These first ancestors of the human race were divinely created by the hand of God. They were probably the most perfect physically, mentally, and morally of any people who have ever lived. And during their lifetime, their children and grandchildren and great-grandchildren had already learned to build cities (Gen. 4:17), raise livestock (Gen. 4:20), make and play musical instruments (Gen. 4:21), and manufacture articles of brass and iron (Gen. 4:22)!

This certainly doesn't sound much like the "cave men" stories we have read, does it? And yet if some atheistic professor should someday find the skull of the fellow I saw up that tree—the professor will probably announce to the world that he has found the missing link! He will point to the sloping forehead, the ridges above the eyebrows, the large jaws and thus "prove" that the fellow lived a gillion years ago! He will call his discovery *Halfwitto Africaneous* and be acclaimed a genius by his fellow "scientists"! Actually, he will simply have found the skull of a human degenerate. No scientist has ever discovered a human skull whose counterpart is not walking around, very much alive, this very moment!

The truth is that God created man in His own image with superior intellect and bodies. So-called "cave men" are degenerates who once knew God but deliberately chose not to glorify Him as God. Their foolish hearts were darkened, their minds were affected and

"Professing themselves to be wise, they became fools"—*Romans 1:22.*

The world did not begin with cave men, but it may well end with them if God allows the world to last much longer!

11

SIMBA, THE AFRICAN LION

It is almost impossible to think of Africa without thinking of the African lion, the king of the beasts. They are not the largest of wild beasts, nor the strongest, nor the fastest, and I am not sure they are the most intelligent. And yet there is not an animal on earth that will challenge the supremacy of the lion in whatever place he has chosen as his domain.

There is something regal about *Simba's* bearing. Perhaps the self-confidence, the nonchalance coupled with the gracefulness of his movements, set him apart from the other jungle beasts.

In color he is grayish-golden. The male is distinguished by a tawny mane on his head, neck, and shoulders. This mane is usually of a darker color than the body to give a two-toned effect. It may be real dark or even black.

The male lion is no small animal. He may be ten feet long from the tip of his nose to the tip of his tufted tail and may weigh four hundred pounds.

He will hunt any time he is hungry but he prefers to hunt at night and sleep during the day. He likes a den in a jumble of rocks.

And when his belly is full, he likes to sprawl out among the rocks or in tall grass.

Lions Live in Family Groups

Usually lions do not live or hunt alone. Where you find one lion, you usually find several consisting of the male and several females and a number of half-grown cubs. The group is called a pride.

As a rule, ole Leo doesn't do enough work to keep in good physical condition. He can run like the wind if he must but he tires quickly. For this reason it is a rare thing that he just plain chases a buffalo or zebra or deer or giraffe until he catches it. But he couldn't probably care less. He intends for his wives to do most of the work, anyway!

When hungry, the pride of lions will usually amble down to the nearest creek or watering hole to see what is on the menu. After they have sized up the situation, the female lions will hide in thickets or tall grass beside several of the trails leading away from the water hole. But they always get *downwind* of the unsuspecting animal on which they intend to dine. When the females are in place, the male will circle around and get *upwind* of the prey. His scent will be carried by the wind down to the deer or zebra or whatever animal they have selected. And just to be sure that this animal is fully aware of Leo's presence, he will urinate and then cough loudly a few times.

By this time, the victim has been thoroughly frightened. He will wheel to run away from Leo not knowing, of course, that regardless of the trail he chooses there is likely to be a welcoming committee in the person of one of the mama lions crouching by the trail. When the deer starts to pass Mama she lets out an earth-shaking roar that almost petrifies the poor beast for a fleeting moment. And that moment is all it takes for the female to put on her tremendous burst of speed that enables her to land on the victim's back and bring it down.

Sometimes the entire family will dine at the spot where the kill was made. Often, however, they will carry or drag the slain beast to some particular spot where they have dined before. Incidentally, the lion is an unusually powerful beast. His strength is phenomenal. Lions have been known to jump a high stockade fence, seize a full-grown goat with their mouths, and then jump back over the fence, carrying the goat. A full-grown lion can half-carry and half-drag a full-grown zebra or bushbuck for long distances with apparent ease.

Sometimes Kill Humans for Food

Like almost any wild animal, the lion is largely unpredictable. As a rule, however, he will not molest another animal or a human being if his belly is full. It is a peculiar thing but deer and zebra and other herbivores seem to sense whether or not they have anything to fear from a lion. When a lion has made a kill and has eaten his fill, these other animals may walk within a few yards of him without apparent apprehension. And the lion will look at the passing animals with complete indifference.

Like most wild animals, *Simba* usually gives men a wide berth. It seems that God has put this instinct in the wildest of beasts. Actually, men are easier to catch and to kill than almost any beast of prey would be. This is probably the reason that an occasional old lion will become a man-eater.

When game is not plentiful, lions are nocturnal hunters. They sleep during the day and then go on the prowl at night. Often, when we traveled late at night, the headlights of the Pie-wagon would shine up the trail on two large eyes that belonged to lions.

And more than once we would be aware that lions were around our camp because of their peculiar cough. Jokingly, I would tell my companions that when I got back to America, I was going to start a home in Arizona for tubercular lions! Imagine my surprise when I found out that those coughing lions really do have tuberculosis!

One night on a jungle road the old Pie-wagon had a flat. While we were fixing it we suddenly heard a peculiar buzzing or rumbling sound. When Austin Paul cocked his ear, listened a minute and then said, "I wonder what is making that noise?" I promptly replied, "It's a baby Noel." Noel, I went on to explain, was our pet lion and the noise we could hear was that of a baby lion, well-fed and content, purring like a kitten. *Bwana* Paul did not know whether to believe me or not until, with a flashlight, we finally spotted the little fellow just eight or ten feet off the trail!

Until the baby lion is several months old he hardly looks like a lion at all. His fur is curly and similar to the wool of a sheep. It is brown in color and the little fellow is spotted! It is not until he is several months old that he sheds his baby fur and becomes the yellow color with which we are all familiar.

I wanted to pick the little fellow up, but I was afraid that his mother might be nearby and she would want to pick me up! So we went about our business of changing the tire while the baby lion watched with interest and buzzed with contentment.

Lion Brings Missionaries to Their Knees in Laughter!

I mentioned my pet lion named Noel. The Princess and I bought her out in El Paso, Texas, when she was just three days old. We raised her on a bottle and she made a wonderful pet. We just loved her! However, when she was about one year old it took about fourteen pounds of horse meat a day to keep her happy, and

I thought every horse on the Ranch was going to have a nervous breakdown! So, we loaned her to the zoo in Memphis, Tennessee.

But Noel was three months old when I left for Africa. I had pictures of Noel and the rest of my family in my wallet and this brought a couple of lovely missionary girls to their knees.

It happened like this—

One day in the Sudan a number of missionaries crowded into the old Pie-wagon to go with us to a gospel service. Two young women, Olive Rawn and Martha Hughell, were seated near me and I was asking them questions about their life in Africa. Several days before, a lion had killed an elderly native in a nearby village and this, of course, was the topic of conversation. But, the two girls told me, one night they had heard a lion in their village and the thoughts of a lion in the same village certainly had frightened them.

"That's nothing," I told them. "The very last day I was home a lion came into my house and jumped right up on the kitchen table!"

With big grins the two girls asked, "What did you do?"

"What did I do? I grabbed her by the tail, dragged her off the table, and put her out the door."

"I'll just bet you did!" one of them said. "I just know you are bothered with lions in Tennessee!"

"It really happened," I protested.

"But it wasn't a real lion," they said.

"Yes, it was," I insisted.

"You don't actually expect us to believe that!"

"But it's the truth," I said. "A real, live, sure-'nuff African lion got in our house and got up on the table and I pulled her down by the tail and put her out the door. That's the honest-to-goodness truth—it really happened."

They wouldn't believe that in a million years, they told me.

"I greatly fear my veracity is doubted," I told them in mock dignity, "and I feel compelled to try to make you believe me. Now, if I do make you believe my story, will you apologize to me on your bended knees?"

If I could make them believe that fantastic story, they said, they would certainly apologize on bended knees. But nothing on earth could ever make them believe a wild tale like that. They changed their minds a minute later, however, when I took my billfold from my pocket and showed them pictures of Noel.

When we reached our preaching destination we jokingly designated a spot of ground as a "mourners' bench" and I invited all present who doubted the word of a preacher to come confess their sins. To the delight of the other missionaries and the howling amusement of the natives, the two young women laughingly fell to their knees in mock apology and I snapped their picture!

I told them I was going to suggest that A.I.M. put the picture on the cover of their little booklet, "We Want Men."

Rendezvous at the Rock

When we were camped on the Semliki River, lions made off with our meat every night. But the night we stayed on the great rock we knew that if the lions took our meat they were going to take us right along with it! That was one night I am not likely to ever forget.

We had been hunting since the middle of the morning and it was now past the middle of the afternoon, and yet neither of my two companions nor I had even fired a shot. The area abounded in game but it just hadn't been our day for seeing it. We were hunting along the edge of the jungle. Fairly open land, like fingers, penetrated into the jungle and these fingers usually connected or intersected to make a network of long, narrow clearings in the jungle's edge.

It must have been about 5:00 o'clock in the afternoon that a long, narrow clearing emptied into a large, round meadow of about ten acres. In the very middle of this large clearing there was a jumble of massive rocks—rocks as large as a church house. On the far side of the clearing we could see two openings in the jungle that led into still other clearings. Since it was getting late, we decided to split up and meet back at this huge jumble of rocks before dark. We would then walk the several miles back to the stream where we had left the Pie-wagon and drive back to the location of the evening's service.

With one of the missionaries and five of the natives, I entered the opening to one of the narrow clearings and in about a quarter of a mile it opened into a large meadow-like area of probably sixty or seventy acres. It was studded with trees but no thick brush. We had walked along slowly and silently for about forty-five minutes without seeing any game of any description. I halted the group to say that I felt we should turn back to the great rock when we spooked a bushbuck. Evidently, the big deer (the "deer" we hunted were actually antelope) had been asleep and the sound of my voice, telling the fellows we had better turn back, had awakened him.

The big buck went streaking off directly in front of us and I dropped him with one lucky shot.

A couple of the natives began dressing the deer when another informed us that, just over the rise and in the edge of the jungle, there was a large herd of buffalo. Telling two of the men to finish with the deer and then to wait for us, the other three natives, the missionary, and I went over the rise to see what we could see. Sure enough, about a half a mile away in the edge of the jungle there was a herd of twelve or fifteen buffalo. Fortunately, we were downwind of them and we were able, by crouching and crawling, to get within two hundred yards of the grazing buffs. Each of us selected a tree to climb in case the situation should get rough; I selected a great big bull, released the safety, and raised the big rifle to my shoulder. It was then I realized that it would be dark in another few minutes. Darkness comes abruptly on the equator and it was already so dark I couldn't see the front sight on my rifle.

I aimed as best I could at the big bull and squeezed the trigger. With the crack of the rifle, the herd stampeded except for the big bull. He fell and, by the time we got to him, so did the darkness.

A Fire in the Sky

The downed buffalo must have weighed two thousand pounds. We decided the best thing for us to do was to leave him there, walk back to meet our companions at the jumble of rocks, and then decide what to do about all that meat. So we walked back to where the two men had finished dressing out the bushbuck, divided it, and each native placed a hunk of meat on his head and shoulders. We then lined up in single file with each one of us holding onto the spear or rifle of the one just in front so that we would not get separated in the darkness.

Slowly we made our way along. A native with the eyes of a cat was first in line and I was next, holding onto the butt of his spear. The going, because of the darkness, was slow. Suddenly the fellow in the lead dropped flat to the ground and I followed suit; and so did all the others behind, for all the world like dominoes fall when they are all on edge and the first one is pushed over against the next.

"*Timbu*," the native whispered. I peered hard into the darkness ahead and then, sure enough, saw the outline of a great elephant between me and the darkened sky. And then I saw another and another. We turned and, on our hands and knees, scooted back a couple of hundred yards. We then tested the wind and began a wide detour of the elephants.

The jungle really comes alive at night when the nocturnal hunters are on the prowl. With all of that fresh, bloody meat we were more than a little uneasy. I suggested that we light torches but this idea was quickly vetoed. A light of any kind is likely to anger an elephant. More than once, I was told, an elephant has been enraged by car lights shining in his eyes and has promptly retaliated by turning the car over and stomping it flat!

Finally the moon came up, and although it was not a bright night, we could see to walk without hanging onto one another's rifles or spears. When we finally came to the place where our large meadow narrowed into a neck in the jungle before opening into the clearing that contained the rocks, we saw a strange sight. High in the sky we could see the leaping flames of a large fire. Our companions had long since returned to the rock and had carried wood to the very top and set it afire that its light could guide us in the darkness!

I fired my six-gun several times and we soon saw flames of fire descending as though coming down from Heaven. Men with torches were climbing down the jumble of rocks. They ran to meet us, helped carry our load of fresh meat, and in another half hour we were all gathered on the top of the great rocks around the fire.

Fresh Meat on the Lions' Table

The other party, having seen no game, had returned to the rock long before sundown. When it became evident we were going to be late in returning, they had carried great stacks of dead wood and dead grass to the top of the highest rock—probably as high above the ground as the steeple on a large church building.

N one of us had eaten since an early breakfast and we were soon busy broiling strips of deer meat over the burning embers. We had no other food of any kind but, even without salt, the meat was delicious and we ate our fill.

The fire had burned down while we ate and talked, and suddenly we were aware of the presence of lions at the base of the rocks far below. It seemed a number of lions had gathered and we could hear them coughing and "talking" to one another. Now, the presence of lions is not too unusual, but for a number of them to gather near the camp and stay there was a bit out of the ordinary.

At first we thought little of it. But it soon became evident that something unusual was going on down there. The big cats were restlessly moving about. Of course, they could smell the freshly killed bushbuck we had carried with us. By the sounds they made— the coughing, an occasional snarl, the throat-rumble or guttural noise that is peculiar to lions—we guessed there were probably five or six in the pride.

We did not become too uneasy until the natives said they could hear the scratching of claw on rock—several of those big tomcats were evidently thinking about joining our party!

We were wondering just how seriously we ought to take the situation, when the scream of a native brought us to our feet with our weapons in our hands. One of our men, carrying his spear, had climbed down eight or ten feet to a great flat rock that must have been sixty feet long and perhaps thirty feet wide. A coming storm had already blacked out the moon and we couldn't see the fellow, but we sure could hear him.

"*Bwana, Bwana*," he screamed, "*opisi* (come)!"

Bwana Paul and I grabbed torches from the fire and made our way down to the fellow as quickly as we could. I have never before or since seen anything like the macabre display seen in the light of our flickering torches. We were standing in the midst of a veritable boneyard. Skulls of bushbuck, *bodi*, and buffalo, with horns still attached, were scattered in a jumble of gleaming well-gnawed bones and tufts of skin and hair!

"What in the world .. .!" I gasped, and then the truth hit both of us like a blow in the belly. Lions evidently used this great jumble of rocks as a lookout for game that came into the surrounding meadow to graze or on the way to and from water. They would leave the rocks, pounce upon their unwary prey, and then bring their kill back to this great flat rock where they could eat their fill in peace. No wonder the lions were restless. Of all the places in Africa to spend the night, we had selected their dining room!

Keep the Fire Burning

We immediately called a council of war. I wanted to throw all of the meat we had down to the lions, but this idea was vetoed immediately. In the first place, some of it might lodge in the cracks after rolling only eight or ten feet, and any lion that came within ten feet of us with the smell of raw meat in his nostrils would likely consider us a definite threat and attack at once. After all, we were usurpers and they resented it. In the second place, who knew but that the meat would just whet their appetites.

The one thing we knew to do was build up that fire and keep it burning brightly. It was the only advantage we had. We needed a bright fire, and yet our supply of wood must last until morning.

But, as it turned out, we had trouble keeping the fire going at all. The thunderstorm that had been brewing suddenly exploded right on top of us. Lightning flashed and thunder rolled and rain came down in torrents.

"Keep that fire going," Austin Paul yelled, "or we will never be able to start it again with everything soaking wet."

A number of us, both black and white, pressed our sides tight together and leaned over the fire in an attempt to shield it from the driving rain. (I did not realize until the morning that in doing this, I had badly blistered my face and had singed off my eyelashes, eyebrows, and most of the hair not covered with my hat.) Others pounded dead wood on the rock to break it open and get the dry rotten centers to throw on the sputtering fire. Others seized armfuls of the grass we had intended as our beds and fed the flames with it.

The storm, while it lasted, was furious. But, like so many thunderstorms of the jungles, it was fairly brief in duration. By guarding the fire with our bodies while feeding it on dry rotten wood, we were able to keep it alive and burning. After the rain stopped we managed, even with wet wood, to get a roaring fire going again.

During the storm, the lions had evidently sought shelter in a den among the rocks. But when the storm passed, they began making their presence heard once more. Presently, a native yelled and hurled his spear down into the darkness. This brought all of us to stand in a semicircle at the edge of the rock. There was nothing to fear at our backs for there the rock fell away in a precipice.

It was a weird situation. I just couldn't believe the lions would actually attack so many of us on the very top of the rock. But the natives thought they would and it was, of course, a distinct possibility. Although three of us had firearms (I stood on the edge of that rock holding two six-shooters and feeling like an utter idiot), the lions still had the advantage. They could see in the darkness and we couldn't. They knew exactly how many of us there were and where we were standing. It was unlikely we would see any of them until he flashed into the circle of firelight.

Like I said, it was a weird and peculiar situation. The natives were positive that the lions would attack. We were tense, but we simply did not believe ole Leo and his family would risk a fight. While we were standing there I told Austin Paul about the two lions that were hiding in the grass and watching the approach of a missionary and a native. One lion finally said to his companion, "I think I'll take vanilla," whereupon the other lion said, "That's okay with me—I like chocolate better anyway."

Bwana Paul exploded with laughter. He doubled over and hollered until I thought he was going to fall headfirst off the rock! In a moment, every native there—although none of them understood a word of English—had joined in the laughter! They stomped, doubled over, and hugged their stomachs as they bellered in laughter.

When *Bwana* Paul tried to interpret the joke, the natives wondered what in the world they had been laughing about. None of them had the vaguest idea as to what vanilla and chocolate were.

We fired our guns into the darkness and, after a bit, posted a couple of guards. The rest of us lay down to try to get a little sleep before daylight. I had hardly closed my eyes when one of the natives let out a bloodcurdling scream and yelled, "*Moto, moto* (death, death)!" All of us jumped to our feet, thinking a lion surely must have seized the fellow. But all we saw was one of the natives nursing his foot. It seems that "*moto*" not only means "death" but "fire." He had thrust his foot too near the fire and had burned his big toe!

We put all of our remaining wood on the fire and then lay down, still soaking wet, to sleep until awakened by the bright rays of the morning sun.

(One large black man seemed to have taken an unusual liking for me. During the entire trip, he had been constantly at my side. Several times, while stalking game, he had offered to carry my rifle. He had been with me when I downed the big buffalo bull. And now, all night long on the rock, he had been constantly by my side and had seemed unusually solicitous for my welfare. It had been he who had gotten the green stick for me to use in broiling meat over the fire, and he had squatted by my side, cooking a strip for himself. When we had finally managed to get some sleep, I was the last one to wake up in the morning because he was squatting on his haunches beside me, using his body to shield my face from the sun. Finally, Austin Paul asked him why he was so sold on me, and the big man replied that several weeks before, in the heat of the day, I had sat down beside him and led him to Christ.)

The Dayspring From on High

The next morning, before broiling strips of deer meat for breakfast, we climbed down to the adjoining flat rock to explore the boneyard we had seen briefly in the light of our torches the night before. Neither missionaries nor natives had ever seen anything like it before.

As we stood in the midst of the bones, I turned to *Bwana* Paul and said, "Do you believe we were in any real danger last night? Do you believe there was any real probability of our bones being spread out here with all these others?"

Bwana Paul thought for a moment and then replied, "I don't think there is any doubt but there was a possibility of the lions attacking us. In fact, I believe they probably would have except for one thing—we had a fire to protect us. Wild beasts are afraid of a fire and it is a rare thing they will come near one. In fact," he continued, "jungle killers do not like daylight, either. You will notice that none of those lions stayed around after it got light."

Good Neighbor, I have thought many times about that night we stayed on that little mountain of massive boulders—the night we stayed on the lions' table. Again and again, I have thought of those hungry, angry lions moving restlessly in the darkness but afraid to attack us because of our fire.

The Bible says, *"Be sober, be vigilant; because your adversary the devil, as a roaring lion, walketh about, seeking whom he may devour"* (I Peter 5:8).

Satan, like a lion, stalks about in the darkness—hungry, angry, vicious—ready to attack!

But, the Bible says, *"For our God is a consuming fire"* (Hebrews 12:29). We read that Jesus is the *"...light of the world..."* (John 8:12). He is our Sun, the Dayspring from on High.

The only protection any of us have from Satan is the Lord Jesus Christ, our Fire. And the only hope any of us have for a world that is lost in the blackness of sin is that soon the Sun of Righteousness shall appear to drive the night away.

12

MR. RUGG AND THE ELEPHANT

His Native Helper Needed a Wife but Did Not Have the "Wealth" With Which to Purchase One. Bwana Rugg Decided to Help by Killing an Elephant and Trading the Tusks for a Bride.

Mr. Rugg (that is not his real name and I have forgotten which mission board he served under) had served several terms in Africa as a missionary. Then, for some reason or other, he returned to the States. But when he heard that a Hollywood film company was going to make a movie in Africa, he applied for a job as interpreter. After all, he said, he had lived in Africa, knew the native dialects, knew the customs, and knew the country. So, he returned to Africa as an advisor in the making of a movie. When the cinema company returned to Hollywood, he remained in Africa.

He was an excellent hunter and when one of his favorite African helpers wanted a wife but did not have the "wealth" with which to buy one, Mr. Rugg decided to help. After all, he reasoned, it would be a fairly simple thing for him to kill an elephant and give the tusks to his friend in order that he might purchase a bride.

Now, let me frankly say that I am scared of wild elephants. A great big bull with crooked tusks, who had already killed two men, charged Austin Paul and me one day, and we just barely escaped with our lives. I am not afraid of lions. I am not afraid of leopards. I am just a little bit afraid of the African buffalo. But the very thought of meeting an angry bull elephant on the trail face to face is enough to scare me silly!

Timbu!

Like I said, Mr. Rugg was a good hunter. He not only knew where to look for elephants, but he knew when to look for elephants. Moreover, he was an excellent shot.

With the native who wanted a wife and, I believe, one other man, he went looking for an elephant with large tusks. And they found exactly what they were looking for on the edge of a large tract of *matete*. He was an enormous bull elephant with great ivory tusks.

In great excitement, the bachelor whispered to Rugg, "*Timbu, Bwana, Timbu* (Elephant, White Boss Man, elephant)!" As they crept closer to the unwary giant, Mr. Rugg noted with satisfaction that the elephant was standing right in the middle of a large game trail. This was great. He would kill the elephant and then drive his jeep right up to the carcass. They would not have to tote the heavy tusks.

Carefully, the three men crept nearer and nearer to the great beast. Finally, when he thought he was close enough, Mr. Rugg raised his high-powered rifle, aimed carefully, and pulled the trigger.

Now, a huge elephant is not the easiest animal in the world to kill. About the only way to kill an elephant instantly is to put a bullet in his brain. But it takes a crack shot—or a mighty lucky one—to do it. The elephant has an enormous skull, and even a steel-jacketed bullet is more likely to be halted or deflected than it is to penetrate the thick skull and enter the brain. But there are two places, each about as large as a silver dollar, that the bullet may hit and kill immediately.

One of these places is in the elephant's forehead. You look the elephant full in the face and imagine that a line is drawn from the root of the left tusk to the corner of the right eye and that another line is drawn from the root of the right tusk to the corner of the left eye. Where these lines cross is that vulnerable spot about as large as a silver dollar. Hit that spot with a steel-jacketed bullet from a high-powered rifle and the elephant will come down. The other vulnerable place is in the opening of the ear. Here again, there is a place about as large as a silver dollar through which a bullet can pass into the brain.

Of course, if the elephant is charging and you are not a good enough shot to hit a spot as small as a dollar—do what I did and run to beat sixty!

Although Mr. Rugg was a crack shot, his bullet went just a little wide of the mark. The elephant, although mortally wounded, trumpeted loudly and dashed into the *matete*.

Dashing forward, the men could hear the elephant crashing through the thick growth of giant grass. I really do not know why they call it grass. It is as large around as a cane fishing pole and may grow as high as fourteen feet.

It was easy to see that the elephant had been hard hit. Blood, gushing from the great beast, had left a crimson trail in his wake.

Bwana Rugg Is Dead!

Turning to his two native trackers, Mr. Rugg told them to follow the blood spoor into the *matete*. Both of them refused. "*Bwana*, " they said, "there is death at the end of that trail. *Timbu* will surely kill us if we follow."

Mr. Rugg was impatient. He reminded the bachelor that the hunt was for his benefit, anyway. Perhaps he was a coward and did not deserve a wife. But neither his coaxing nor criticism nor reminder of rewards could persuade either of the two natives.

Finally, in anger, he told both of them that they were cowardly babies and not men. He ordered them to go home at once. And this they did.

Some hours later they walked into the village to announce that *Bwana* Rugg was dead. He had been killed, they said, by a wounded bull elephant.

Other missionaries were summoned at once and they, with a number of natives, went back to look for the hunter.

As it turned out, the natives had been absolutely right. Mr. Rugg *was* dead, and he *had* been killed by the wounded elephant.

The Spoor Told the Story

They found the great elephant dead in the middle of the very trail where he had been standing when he had been shot. Mr. Rugg, with a horrible hole through his body just above the belt, was lying some twenty feet away.

By looking at the trail of blood, the men knew exactly what had happened as clearly as though they had been eyewitnesses.

First, there was the spoor of blood the elephant had left behind when he had gone crashing into the *matete*. He had gone for some two hundred yards and then had stopped and stood still for several minutes. This could be determined because there was a great pool of blood at the end of the trail. The elephant had then retraced his steps until he was no more than fifty or sixty yards from the place where he had been shot. There the great beast had turned and walked off the trail for about ten feet. Then he turned around and stood facing his original trail. Here the cunning beast had quietly stood waiting for his enemy to follow. The great pool of blood there gave mute testimony to the fact that Mr. Rugg must have followed the trail very slowly and cautiously. Of course, it was easy enough to see where the elephant had gone because the tall grass had been pressed flat under his feet. But a man is not an elephant, and it is very difficult to move through this stuff. I know because I have tried it more than once.

The hunter, moving slowly, strained his eyes to see ahead. It had not occurred to him that the elephant might double back in his own tracks. In his anxiety to see the great beast while it was still some distance away, he did not see it at all until he reached the place where the elephant was quietly waiting just at the side of the trail!

It is doubtful if Mr. Rugg saw the elephant even then until the great beast, trumpeting in anger and pain, charged! The tusk went in his body near his backbone just above the belt and came out in front just above the belt.

The great beast then raised his head, holding the skewered man high in the air. With the hunter's blood bathing the wounded elephant's face, the great beast walked back down the trail to the clearing. Standing on the very place where he had been shot, the beast slung his head, throwing the missionary some twenty feet away. Slowly, then, *Timbu* sank to the ground and expired.

They Paid a Great Price—for What?

Many times I have meditated upon the fate of Mr. Rugg and the elephant—the hunter and the hunted who killed one another. I feel sorry for both of them.

I regret that the great beast was killed. He was a splendid animal with beautiful ivory tusks and tremendous size. He was possessed by an indomitable spirit.

When Mr. Rugg's bullet slammed into the huge beast he ran, crashing headlong into the stand of giant grass. The hunter, of course, felt the elephant was trying to escape—which was exactly what *Timbu* wanted him to think. Actually, the elephant probably realized almost at once that he had sustained a mortal hurt. Blood was spurting from the wound like water from a faucet. Almost at once, he began to feel weak and faint and deathly sick. With all of his being, he wanted to elude the man with the death-dealing gun and then lie down and rest.

But this he did not do! He had a job to do before he died—and he did it. As far as he was concerned he had been attacked without cause; and he obviously felt he must, before he died, destroy this enemy of elephants.

So—although deathly sick and in great pain—the great pachyderm deliberately retraced his steps to the place he had elected to patiently wait, beside the trail he had made for Mr. Rugg. There, he not only resisted the strong desire to lie down and rest but evidently held death at bay until he had an opportunity to accomplish the thing he felt he simply must do before he died.

In this he was magnificent!

I am not speaking of revenge which is—in man—weak, wicked, and unworthy. Rather, I am speaking of the elephant's persistence. Tenacity is an admirable trait in any man or beast. The big tusker was determined to finish his course in spite of sacrifice, suffering, danger, and death.

Many a layman, missionary, pastor, and evangelist could learn a lesson from this big fellow's example. Entirely too many of God's servants lack stick-ability. Thank God for the ones who put their hand to the plow and never look back! The ones who cannot be bullied, bluffed, bribed, or buffeted into quitting!

As for Mr. Rugg—I greatly admire courage, and evidently he was a brave man. And yet, I sadly feel that when it came to courage he was a spendthrift. He used his courage recklessly. He used it ill-advisedly. He didn't get his money's worth. His courage was not used profitably.

Many a cowardly preacher, afraid of suffering, quits the ministry. Mr. Rugg was certainly no coward, but he, too, lost his ministry when he lost his life. What a tragedy that this man, with boldness so needed by missionaries in the Dark Continent, should have lost his life so needlessly.

13

PYGMIES

A Safari Into the Mysterious "Dark Forest," One of the World's Vast, Partially-Unexplored Jungles, in Search of the "Little People"

When *Bwana* Paul invited me to come to the Belgian Congo, he stressed the fact that he wanted me to go on safari into the great African jungle called the Dark Forest to search for Pygmies.

No one knows just how many Pygmies there are in the Dark Forest. In the first place, they are an elusive little people. In the second place, the Dark Forest has not been fully explored. Of course, missionaries have known of some of the Pygmy tribes for many years, but the missionaries are already overworked. They simply have more to do than they can get around to doing. It was hoped that my going into the jungle would spread interest among both missionaries and the folks back home.

So there came upon a day that Austin Paul, Claudon Stauffacher, and I left a small village on the edge of the great jungle and made our way inland. We drove the Pie-wagon down a game trail for

135

as many miles as we could. At the end of the broad trail we found about forty natives waiting to carry our gear further into the jungle. We made up quite a procession. Four natives with machetes took the lead widening the narrow little game trail that wound its way through the jungle. Behind us came about forty natives carrying on their heads and backs the provisions we would need in the jungle. Some carried large yellow tarpaulins that we later stretched between trees to make a shelter from the rain. Others carried baskets of foodstuffs balanced on their heads. Others carried cooking utensils, ammunition for the rifles, etc.

The Deserted Village

It was late on an afternoon that we ran into a broad, well-traveled trail that led us to the Pygmy village. It was located in a jungle clearing about 50 yards wide and perhaps 150 yards long. Giant trees, so tall they seemed almost to reach the sky, completely surrounded the clearing. Sprinkled over two-thirds of the clearing were tiny round huts covered with banana leaves. The leaves had begun to turn brown and each hut looked, for all the world, like one-half a grapefruit lying face down on the ground! Each hut had one small entrance, so small and so low that even Pygmies had to get on their hands and knees to enter.

There were no huts at the end of the village entered by our trail.

We walked slowly into the clearing, not knowing what to expect. The natives carrying our gear dumped our stuff down at the empty end of the clearing and then gathered around *Bwana* Paul, *Bwana* Stauffacher, and me. We had been wondering what kind of a reception we would get, but we now realized we weren't going to get any reception at all! The village seemed to be completely deserted. Two of the natives on our team walked slowly down through the clearing, looking into each hut. They made the circle and came back, confirming the fact that the village was, indeed, deserted.

I suggested that perhaps we should have left our group of carriers several hundred yards back down the trail until we had entered the village alone and made friends. My companions assured me, however, that the Pygmies had doubtless been aware of our number and destination while we were still miles away!

As we had approached the village, they had—literally—high-tailed it for the tall timber! After all, we were not only strangers but very strange strangers. Few of them had ever seen a white man before. They had gone into hiding until they could find out what we were up to.

Getting Acquainted

We set up camp in the uninhabited end of the clearing. Our shelter was a large tarp suspended on ropes that were tied between trees. This provided a roof over our heads to shelter us from the rain that fell every night. We slept on inflated rubber mattresses. Claudon made a rude table by tying a framework of limbs together with vines and covering it with a row of round branches about the size of broom handles. We put this table in front of our shelter and used it for eating and for writing.

We paid off our carriers and sent them back to Oicha, keeping with us only the four natives who were members of our revival team and a couple of extra men to help with the cooking.

Just before dark, one of the natives said something in a low voice to Austin Paul, and he told me that several Pygmy men had come out of the jungle and were hiding behind huts at the far end of the clearing. *Bwana* Paul cautioned me not to make any sudden moves no matter what happened and, should the Pygmies expose themselves to our view, to act as though we had known they were there all the time.

We made a fire and began preparing our supper. I think all of us were a bit excited at the prospect of just being there. I know that I was. After all, the Princess and I had sold our home in Wheaton to make it possible for me to fly across the Atlantic and journey halfway around the world in order to have the privilege of telling these little people what the Lord Jesus Christ had done for me and what He would do for them.

Darkness, as always seems to be the case near the equator, fell quickly. We continued preparing supper, wondering how many eyes were staring at us from the darkness and wondering what was going on in the minds of those who watched. Presently, Austin Paul spoke, in *Bangala*, to one of our natives. "Tell them," he said, "that we are friends and have come to this village in peace. We are about to eat and would be honored if they would come and eat with us."

Our native looked out into the darkness of the clearing and, without raising his voice, did as Austin Paul had bade him. For perhaps another fifteen minutes, there was no sign or sound that anyone was even out there at all. Then a tiny little brown man, old and wrinkled and wearing a monkey-skin cap and a loincloth, walked into the light of our fire. His name was *Tarasi* (a French word meaning "Ditch") he told us. We never did learn how he had acquired the name. He said he was very wise and hinted that he would be a very valuable man for us to have as a friend. Austin Paul courteously replied, using our native as an interpreter, that we were very happy to have the friendship of one so wise and helpful.

Suddenly, I was startled to realize that several other Pygmies, armed with bows and arrows and spears, were standing just a few feet behind us on our side of the campfire! While *Tarasi* had been speaking, they had silently approached. We began eating as Austin

Paul quietly told them that we were friends who had come with gifts for everyone in the village. Except for *Tarasi*, none of them spoke either to us or among themselves. They silently accepted the little trinkets we gave them and examined them without any expression. *Tarasi*, however, continued to talk, boasting and bragging upon himself. When we had finished eating we were suddenly aware of the fact that every last one of them had disappeared as silently and suddenly as they had appeared.

I must admit that I slept rather uneasily that night. I had heard all manner of stories about their poisoned arrows and spears. Oddly enough, we had never at any time or place mapped any strategy as to what we would do if we should be attacked except for the agreement that if it was ever a matter of "kill or be killed"—we would be killed.

The next morning, the same few Pygmies slipped back into the clearing and quietly walked up and sat down around our campfire while we were preparing breakfast. They did not accept our invitation to eat but simply stood or squatted around, looking at our gear and occasionally talking among themselves. They stayed around the camp all day. Again and again, without success, we tried to engage them in conversation. When we asked where the rest of the Pygmies were, they would not even answer. Again, that evening, they disappeared silently into the jungle.

But, after several days, we did gain their warm friendship. It happened in a totally unexpected and unplanned manner....

One afternoon, some large red apes appeared in the tall trees at our end of the clearing. The apes, weighing about thirty-five pounds each, chattered and scolded as they peered down at us from their dizzying heights. The little Pygmy men excitedly picked up their bows and arrows. But the distance was too great. If they shot they would only lose their arrows. But the little fellows excitedly talked among themselves; and our natives related their conversation to Austin Paul, who passed the word on to me. The little fellows wanted the apes for food.

Claudon and I picked up rifles and each of us quickly killed two of the red apes. As the monks came crashing down, the little brown men were really excited. How wonderful that we could kill the apes without arrows or spears or even climbing the trees! We gave them the apes and told them that if they would come back the following day and hunt with us, we would kill enough apes for the entire village to have a feast.

Hunting Apes in the Jungle

The next morning, eighteen men and boys came to hunt with us. They went into the jungle to locate tribes of apes and came back to lead us to them.

Now, I have gone hunting hundreds of times in my life, but this was a new experience for me. Just going through the jungle was, in itself, an ordeal for me. Where the little people could scamper I had to stoop over and almost crawl through the vines and dense vegetation. In minutes, I was soaking wet with water that fell from every shaken leaf and from sweat in the steaming jungle. At first I was afraid of snakes and tried to check every one of the thousands of vines I had to crawl through. Soon, however, I just worried about trying to get through the undergrowth! I quickly developed a rip-roaring backache and my temper was such that it would have been plain bad news for any snake that had tackled me!

I managed to get along very well until we came to a jungle stream with high banks. It was here that this Napoleon met his Waterloo.

Years before, a giant tree had fallen across the little river. Now, covered with moss and slime, it made a bridge on which the

Pygmies ran and danced across. I stepped upon the tree and stared intently at the muddy water fourteen feet below, wondering how many crocodiles were lurking just below the surface. However, I had no misgivings as I began walking across.

But in the very center of the stream my boots slipped! I grabbed at branches but they were old and rotten and broke. I waved my arms frantically trying to keep my balance, but it was a losing battle! I went off backwards and fell fourteen feet to land, with a terrific splash, in the river. Of course, all the way down I had only one thought—*crocodiles!* I wondered how many of them would be waiting with their mouths open to catch me! I was somewhat relieved that nothing grabbed me as I went under but, as I fought my way back to the surface, I realized that the big splash would surely bring a number of crocs on the run. In spite of the fact that I was not only fully clothed but wearing boots, I made it to the far bank in jig time.

There were some Pygmies at the top of the bank laying on their bellies, and supported with their spears, other Pygmies who were half-way down the bank. The latter held their spears down to me and I seized them, and they helped me in reaching the top. In all this time, incredibly, not one single crocodile appeared!

When I was safe, but winded, on the bank the little hunters exploded with laughter. Evidently, it was the funniest thing they had ever seen; and they rolled back and forth on the ground, flailing the air with their arms and legs as they screamed with belly laughs!

Again and again that day, one or another of the little rascals would throw down his weapons and pantomime my disaster, climaxing the flailing of arms and staggering with a big fall backwards to the ground and, on his tummy, the frantic swim toward the shore! When we returned to their clearing, I think everyone of the eighteen acted it out a dozen times for the benefit of the entire Pygmy village! And, of course, the story lost nothing in the telling. Every time they told the story, their audience would go into gales of delighted laughter. (Incidentally, we had to cross that same infernal "bridge" on our way back, and I made it without incident. My heart was in my throat and I was scared half to death—but I made it.)

In the meantime, our scouts had located a large tribe of apes; and in the hunt that followed, Claudon and I killed exactly thirty of the large red beasts. I'll never forget the sight we made as the little men carried those apes on poles back into camp that afternoon.

The Feast-Ying!

Runners went scooting down the jungle trails to tell those still in hiding that the giant whites were friendly and that they were going to have a great feast. By ones, twos, and dozens the little folks came pouring into the village at sundown. And what a night they had!

Men skinned raw monkey tails and gave them to little boys who ate them like corn on the cob! Fires were lighted, hair was singed off the apes, and then the cooking began. Some put apes on spits and as soon as the outer flesh was half-cooked, they tore it off and ate it while cooking the remainder. A toothless old man was boiling a grinning monkey head in a pot and tearing off shreds of meat from time to time.

The stench of burning hair and blood and entrails and flesh was sickening to me, but obviously it was a heavenly aroma to the Pygmies.

Until late that night, the cooking fires burned and the little folks ate…and ate and ate until all thirty of the apes were completely devoured! And I do mean "completely"—the Pygmies ate everything except the hair, hide, and bone. The tummies of the Pygmies were round and bulging. To them this is beautiful and a sign of prosperity. They are immensely proud of big bellies. They like to *ying* (stuff themselves with food until their bellies bulge) and cast admiring glances at one another's protruding abdomens.

Many Congo natives have large, bloated stomachs probably caused by malnutrition. But Austin Paul and I jokingly said we had made the scientific discovery of the age—we had learned why Congolese had such large stomachs—they were in the "Bulgin'" Congo!

Life in the Pygmy Village

The Pygmies slept late the following morning; but when they finally began to wake up and move around, they were in high good humor. The village was a beehive of good-natured activity. We were now regarded as good friends, and the little people were interested in everything we did.

One little warrior who had quite a reputation as a marksman with bow and arrow, challenged me to a shooting contest. He with his bow and arrow, and me with my six gun. We drew a target on a tree and I easily proved to be the better shot. Every time I fired the pistol the villagers laughed and shouted with delight.

Another man went into the jungle to strip the bark from a tree, with which he made me some bark cloth for clothing. I still have the cloth and the piece of elephant tusk he used to pound the bark with.

A large, overgrown boy begged the chief to give him a wife. Although the youngster was as large as most of the men, the chief felt he was still too young to take care of a woman. As a test, the chief told the boy to see how quickly he could climb to the top of a nearby giant tree. The boy scampered easily to the very top of the tree and then hurried back down again. I never did know if he got the wife or not.

The chief ordered some of the little women to make me a good house. He wanted me for a brother, he said, and would prepare me a house next to his. It took these tiny women forty-five minutes to cut the poles and tie them into a framework with vines and then cover it with banana leaves. It looked for all the world like a green, leafy igloo. I crawled in and tried it on for size, but told the chief I would sleep with my friends for they would be lonesome without me.

The Pygmies ate only one big meal a day and that was in the evening. While the food was cooking, little men would beat the drums and the entire village would dance around and around in a circle, swaying, stomping, and singing for all the world like a rock-and-roll group!

Frustration!

The evening following the great feast, we invited everyone to our "house" for gospel services. Everyone in the village came and sat on the ground before our fire. The men sat in one group, women in another. Children and dogs were everywhere.

As long as our four natives and Mr. Paul played on the trumpets, the Pygmies listened with interest. But when Mr. Paul or Mr. Stauffacher tried to preach, the service became really informal! Women talked, men talked, kids wrestled, dogs fought…and chaos reigned.

The next day—and the next—it was the same. They liked us and were friendly, but they simply were not interested in the Gospel. It was strange to them. Besides, Pygmies—like most of us—are inclined to be mentally lazy, and they simply did not want to do any serious thinking.

We were just heartsick. After spending so much money, working our heads off, risking jungle perils, and suffering malaria, we had finally actually contacted the Pygmies and had made friends with them. But we had not been able to even explain the Gospel to a one of them.

Finally, Austin Paul and Claudon decided that I should try to preach to the Pygmies. I protested that it would take an extra interpreter because I would have to speak in English (Texan) and have Austin put that into *Bangala* and a native put that into Pygmy language. But they insisted that I couldn't do any worse than they had done.

I walked out of the clearing into the jungle and spent the day in prayer. And God heard and answered my prayer. When it was time for the service that night, I knew exactly what to do and how to do it.

"That Red Book Can Talk!"

That night when all of the little people had gathered as usual before our campfire, I put more wood on the fire to make it brighter than usual. Then, I put our camp table before the fire and my red Bible on the table.

Facing the group, I began to speak (through the two interpreters, of course). "Where are your fathers?" I asked.

They looked at one another and I repeated my question, "Where are your fathers?"

"This man is my father, *Bwana*—and there is mine—and mine," they said. I pointed to some of the very old men and asked, "Where are your fathers?"

"They are dead," they replied.

"But where are they?" I wanted to know.

"We buried them in the jungle."

"All right," I said, "they died and you buried them. But where are they right now?"

They looked at me in bewilderment. Finally, someone spoke up and said, "*Bwana*, when our fathers die and we bury them, we know their spirit goes someplace but no man knows where."

"I know where they are," I told them to their astonishment.

A chorus of *ohs* and *ahs* and grunts came from both the men and the women. Finally, the chief stood up and said, "*Bwana Machelli* (Rice), you are a stranger here," he said. "How could you know where our fathers are?"

I turned in the firelight and dramatically pointed to the Bible on the table. "See that red Book," I said. "It can talk! *Munga Baba Yeato* (The Sky God Father or Heavenly Father) gave that Book to me, and that Book has told me where your fathers are!"

A murmur of excitement spread over the group. I waited a moment and then said, changing the subject abruptly, "How many men want to go hunting again?" Several said that they did but there wasn't much enthusiasm. They were talking and gesturing and pointing at the red Bible on the table.

Again I asked how many would like to go hunting, but there was still little response. Finally, one man stood up and asked me, "*Bwana*, does that Book truly tell about our fathers?" I assured him again that the Book could talk and that it had already told me where their fathers were!

Again a buzz of excitement went through the congregation. Then another man stood and motioned for everyone to be quiet. He looked at the Bible on the table, cocked his head to one side, and listened intently. Finally, he said, "*Bwana*, I don't hear that Book saying anything!"

The others began murmuring in agreement when I motioned for everyone to be quiet.

"When you go to hunt," I said to the men, "do you sometimes leave a sign on the trail to tell other hunters which way to go or if you have found game?"

Of course, they all nodded in agreement. They often made signs that "talked." I then picked up the Bible, opened it, and said, "Do you see all of these little black things? They are signs that God has given to tell us what He wants us to know! They are words, and they have told me where your fathers are!"

I put the Bible back on the table and said, "Now, how many of you men want to go hunting with me tomorrow?"

But no one was interested in hunting. Many of them, men, women and children, were standing and peering intently at the Bible on the table. All of them were talking excitedly. Soon one little man stood to his feet and asked the inevitable question, "*Bwana Machelli*, if that Book tells where our fathers are, will you tell us what it says?"

I appeared to think it over for a bit and then said I hardly thought I should. "You see," I explained, "God is a great God and people should be very quiet and thoughtful when someone is telling His Words. My friends have tried to talk to you again and again, but you would not listen. The women talk, talk, talk and the children fight and the dogs bother and the men want to go hunting. So," I said, "I will not tell what God's Book says to people who are not very quiet and thoughtful. Let us talk about hunting."

But no one had any interest in hunting. Again and again, men stood to ask where I had gotten the Book of God, if it truly told where their fathers were, and if I would read it to them. And every time I came back to the same thing—people should be quiet when the Chief speaks and God was more important than all chiefs.

Finally, as I knew he would, the chief stood and said, "*Bwana,* we will be quiet and listen if you will only tell us what God's Book says."

I thought about it for a moment and then agreed to read from God's Book if everyone would be quiet and attentive.

Man alive, but business really did pick up at that! Men went to their wives and shook their fists in their faces and demanded that they shut up talking and be absolutely silent. Men picked up boys and girls, gave them a sharp spat, and sat them down again, telling them not to move and not to say a word. Then they ran all of the dogs out of camp before sitting themselves down and listening attentively.

I have never had a more attentive audience in all my life!

Adam and Eve in Eden

As I looked beyond the flickering firelight at the crowd of Pygmies sitting in that clearing beneath the stars, I prayed that God would help. I realized that none of these had ever heard of a Bible, had never heard of Christ, had never heard of Heaven or Hell or salvation. I did not know how an experienced man would have begun, but I felt sure I knew where God wanted me to begin that night. So, I opened my Bible at the story of Creation. After all, that's where the Bible begins! I read the story of Adam and Eve, explaining as I read.

That first evening, I read the second chapter of Genesis and then closed the Bible, although Pygmy after Pygmy stood and requested that I read more. I told them, however, that I would continue reading in the morning. Far into the night the little fellows talked and talked and talked about *Adomi* and *Eva* and the wonderful jungle of Eden!

That night *Bwana* Paul, *Bwana* Claudon, and I went to our beds very happy men. We felt sure that God had given us the minds and hearts of these little people and that He was going to do a wonderful work among these small citizens of the jungle.

When the Morning Came

I was the first of our group to wake up the following morning. I raised up to a sitting position to take a look at the brand-new day—and almost jumped out of my skin! The entire village was again sitting on the ground in front of our shelter! The men were seated together, the women together, and the children sitting among them. They were as quiet as the proverbial little mice, and for a moment I wondered if they had even gone to bed at all! When I sat up, grins spread over their faces. I woke up the other two men and when they sat up, they were as dumbfounded as I.

With dignity the chief stood to his feet and said, "*Bwana Machelli*, you said you would let the Book of God speak to us again the following day. It is now the following day, and we have come to hear what God wants us to know."

I quickly pulled on my boots, washed up and, with that red Bible in my hand and a song in my heart, joined my two companions for the service. Again I read and spoke, explaining how sin and death had come to mankind through Adam and Eve. I spoke the next several times also and told how Jesus Christ, the Son of God, had come into the world to save sinners. In the course of the messages, the little people learned the whereabouts of their fathers who had gone on before.

Tarasi, the First Convert

One night as I was talking of the love of God and how He had sent Jesus to die for us, old *Tarasi*, the little old man in the monkey-skin cap who had been the very first Pygmy we had met, stood to his feet.

"*Bwana*," he said in his thin voice, "I thought it must be something like that. Many times I have climbed the highest tree and have looked far into the sky, trying to see God. I felt sure He must be up there someplace. And again and again I have called, 'God, are You there? Can You hear me? Do You see little old *Tarasi*? God, I am afraid—come and help *Tarasi*.' But," the odd old fellow continued, "I never could hear Him answer me a word. I thought God surely must have some way of helping poor old *Tarasi*…I am glad to hear of Jesus and to know that He died for me…I thought it must be something like that!"

So old *Tarasi* was our first convert and his son, *Gabani*, was our second.

Two years later, I was informed that a church had been established among this tribe of Pygmies. It was hard for me to realize that some of these small, brown, almost-naked jungle people were now testifying to other Pygmy tribes of the grace of God that brings salvation through our Lord Jesus Christ. In all the world today there are only a few—perhaps five or six—Pygmy churches. I am grateful to God that I was privileged to be present at the beginning of this one.

14

THE VALLEY OF THIRST

Far Away, High on the Valley's Rim, We Could See the Palm Trees That Looked Like Tiny Matches Against the Sky, but Beneath Those Palm Trees Were Canteens of Water…and That Water Meant the Difference Between Life and Death

Just after four o'clock in the morning, we parked the Pie-wagon in a cluster of tall palm trees. We were high on the rim of a valley that stretched long and wide below us. Daylight comes early on the Congo equator, but it was still dark in the valley so far below.

Austin Paul and I and the eight natives climbed out of the Pie-wagon and began checking our hunting gear. *Bwana* Paul and I loaded our high-powered rifles and I strapped my Magnum six-shooter around my waist. The natives tested their spear heads to be sure that they were firmly in place.

A few minutes later, Austin Paul decided it was light enough for us to begin making our way to the floor of the valley below. Grass grew waist high down the steep slope and it was sopping wet from the heavy night dews. We held our rifles above our heads with one hand as we began making the long and often painful descent. I say often painful because again and again, my feet slipped out from under me and I skidded lickety-split on my backside until I could grab another handful of grass and get myself stopped!

By the time we finally reached the floor of the valley, I was drenched to the skin from the droplets of dew that covered every blade of the tall grass.

Although there was no stream of water in the valley, there were numerous seep holes, Mr. Paul explained, where animals could drink. The place was alive with game, and we expected to kill as many large bushbucks as we needed within an hour's time. The main problem was to get the game back up out of the canyon. That, however, was why we had brought the eight natives along.

Big Game for Big Crowds

When Austin Paul wrote and told me what to bring with me to Africa, he said I must be sure and bring a high-powered game rifle. But I vetoed the suggestion. I love to hunt but I was not going to Africa to hunt for big game. I was going to hunt for souls and I wanted to put all of my enthusiasm and energy into the soul-winning campaigns. So, I decided to take only a powerful new Magnum six-shooter. I figured this would be all the protection I would need against wild animals.

But as soon as we started out on the revival trail in Africa, I realized that Austin Paul had been right and I had been wrong. I learned the hard way that it is a long distance between supermarkets in the African jungles and bush. Early in life I had acquired the habit of eating often and much—and if I was going to keep that habit, it was necessary that I help bring in the game that would put meat on the table.

And we tried to have meat for all the people who came on the first day of each revival campaign. We usually began these campaigns on Monday night. Several days before, we would send out runners who would say to the people, "A tall man named Rice has come across the waters in a big bird. He has a message straight from GOD. He will tell us what God wants us to know. Bring all of your wives and children and food and stay for one week."

How the people came! Long lines of people from every direction. Women with baskets on their heads and babies tied to their backs. Children walking single file behind their parents. They came by the dozens, by the hundreds, and even by the thousands!

It was like the camp meetings of America's early days. The population of entire villages came! I have never preached to so many nor seen so many conversions in the same length of time in my life. They came for five services a day, sitting on the ground, usually in the open air.

On Sunday night we would close one revival. On Monday we would travel to the next, often hunting game as we traveled. We always tried to have a couple of buffalo or half-dozen bushbucks to divide among the natives the first Monday afternoon. Although game lives in Africa in abundance, it is difficult to kill with bow and arrows or spears. Accordingly, most natives do not get enough meat, and they were always pleased when they had meat to flavor their "feasts" when they arrived at the revival location.

"Sweeping" the Valley

When we reached the valley floor, it was agreed that Austin Paul and four spearmen would walk one half mile toward the further side. I allowed him fifteen minutes and then began walking slowly down the valley toward a distant spot on the horizon.

Usually *Bwana* Paul and I had good luck on our hunts. But this simply wasn't our day. We saw very little game, probably because the breeze was constantly changing directions. Wild animals have a keen sense of smell, and when they get the scent of a man they usually put on a disappearing act that would make Houdini look like an amateur. What little game we did see was usually a half-mile or more away—a distance too great for accurate shooting.

At the end of two hours the heat was oppressive and I had begun to be in physical distress. Shortly after arriving in Africa I had contracted malaria. The old-time missionaries all knew it was malaria; but the regional missionary doctor, a young Englishman, *knew* it could not be malaria because I had not been there long enough. So, he refused to treat me for malaria. By the time I got around to an old-time missionary doctor several weeks later and a simple blood test was taken, the situation had become rather alarming. I suffered from dysentery and lived hourly with nausea.

It is not a very nice thing to talk about, but I just may have broken the world's record for regurgitating! As fantastic as it sounds, more than once while preaching I was forced to leave the platform to run and vomit and then woud rush back to the platform without ever missing a word or delaying the service! You see, I always had to preach through an interpreter. Sometimes there would be five or six or seven interpreters lined up with me on the platform. I would shout a sentence and hold the gesture. I spoke in English. Austin Paul would translate from English into *Bangala*. A native next to Mr. Paul would translate from *Bangala* into *Kingwana*. The next man would change from *Kingwana* into *Lugbari*, and so on. After I had shouted a verse of Scripture or made a remark in English, I would leave the platform and run around back of the

Pie-wagon to throw up. Then I would rush back on the platform and be ready for the next statement in the sermon!

So after walking for two hours, I was suffering from a blinding headache. We had not eaten any breakfast that morning, and I had not taken a drink of water. By six o'clock the heat was oppressive, my head was throbbing, and I was weak and nauseated. I asked the warriors with me if any of them had canteens of water, and they told me that the men with Austin Paul were carrying the canteens.

We walked another hour and then another. It was about 9:30 when I finally decided I simply could not go any further without water. And yet, I hesitated to send a runner to Austin Paul. So often a man will be stalking game when a runner dashes up to ask some question and it will spook the game and cause the hunter to miss the shot. About 9:30, however, I decided that game or no game, I had been foolish to wait even this long without water. I motioned one of the almost naked spearmen to me and was about to send him to find Austin Paul and water when another of my men, scouting a few yards ahead, whispered excitedly,

"*Opisi, Bwana, bodi!*"

"Come, Mr. Boss," he had said, "I see a deer."

The Longest Shot of the Day

The native, perhaps twenty yards ahead of me, was kneeling behind a large ant hill that was four or five feet high. Crouching, I made my way to him and peered over the mound. But I didn't see any deer anywhere on the ground that sloped up ahead of us.

"*Oya azi*, " I whispered. Roughly, this means "how many;" but he understood that I was asking how far away the deer was. He replied something that I did not understand and then took his spear and aimed it as though it were a gun. I followed the sight of the spear and finally saw the *bodi*.

It was a small deer facing us. He was about 325 yards away (Austin Paul later stepped it off); and at that distance, looked no larger than the edge of my hand.

I motioned to the native that we should try to get closer, but he shook his head in disapproval. Picking up a handful of dust, he let it sift slowly between his fingers. The wind was changing and, in another moment, would be at our backs, blowing our scent directly to the deer. It was either take a shot now or get no shot at all.

The native slowly climbed on the ant hill and thrust the point of his spear in the clay. I slipped up beside him, knelt on one knee, put my left hand around the spear, and rested the barrel of the rifle on that hand. I knew it was a long shot for plain peep sights and even a crack shot would probably miss, and I am certainly no crack shot.

I took careful aim, held my breath for a moment to hold the gun more steadily, and squeezed the trigger.

The deer jumped into the air, turned, and disappeared in the knee-high grass. *He was down!*

My four men ran forward to begin dressing the deer. Presently, from my right, I heard shouts and Austin Paul and his four men quickly approached. "I knew you had made a kill," *Bwana* Paul said, "because you shot only once."

I had sat down on the ant hill and *Bwana* Paul noticed, at a glance, that I was about all in. He asked me if I had drunk any water.

I thought he was joking because Mr. Paul has a rare and wonderful sense of humor. He was usually very cheerful under the most trying and exasperating circumstances—one of the greatest morale builders I have ever known in my life.

Right now, however, I was too sick to appreciate humor.

"Don't joke, *Bwana*," I told him. "I've never been so sick in my life. Please call the native that has the canteens."

Austin Paul looked at me incredulously. "I'm not joking," he said. "Don't you have the water?"

It turned out that neither of us had the water canteens. They had been left behind in the Pie-wagon that was several miles and several hours away.

"Bill," *Bwana* Paul said, "this could be mighty serious, but I think we will make it back all right. I know the natives will because they do not suffer from the broiling heat like we do. Besides, they find stuff to drink that would kill us.

''Now, Bill, none of us are going to wait on the other. We are all going to start out, but if you can't keep up, we are not going to wait on you and we are not going to help you. But we will come back for you as soon as we can.

"Whatever you do—don't panic!"

I unloaded my rifle and handed it to one of the spearmen to carry. I unbuckled my gun belt and strapped it around the neck and under the arm of another. And then we started out.

I brought up the rear of the column. We began moving at a steady walk. It had been a long shot when I hit the deer, but I had a feeling that hitting those canteens was going to be the longest shot of the day.

And I was determined to make it.

Where Was Lazarus?

I don't believe I could describe that walk. It was a nightmare of horror. Part of the time I was in a daze. Part of the time I felt as if I were walking in my sleep and actually wondered if I were. There were many times when I would feel a *thud* and then notice that my face was in the grass and it would take me several moments to realize that I had fallen again.

It seemed that I was always getting behind the other men—sometimes because of falling down. There were times I had to stop because of my sickness. Then I would walk fast and even trot in an effort to catch up. There was no trail to follow, and I was so afraid that I would lose sight of the others and not know which direction to go. (Actually, Mr. Paul had sent two men on ahead to get water and come back with it and these two natives actually did get lost! We didn't see them again until late that afternoon.)

Every time I stumbled and fell it was sheer agony to make myself get back on my feet and begin walking again. As soon as I realized I had fallen, I would pull first one knee and then the other under my belly, then force myself up on my hands and knees and then onto my feet. Sometimes I would stay on my knees for a minute or so, trying to rest. At one such time, the native who had my rifle came running back to me. He excitedly pointed and there, just a few yards away, were two giant bushbucks staring at me. The native tried to hand me the rifle so I could shoot them. It was ironic. I motioned the native away as I whispered through bloody lips, *Boyo, te.*" (Literally, yes, no. Meaning, "Yes, I positively will not!")

Bloody lips? Yes. I cannot explain it, but my lips had swollen enormously and then had begun to split open.

I had never before known what it was to be *really* thirsty. Oh, again and again I have ridden or walked for hours without water and have badly wanted a drink. But never in my life before had my entire body actually suffered for lack of water.

My lips were swollen and parched and split. My tongue, too, was so swollen that it seemed to fill my entire mouth. My mouth was dry. I could feel no moisture with either my tongue or a finger.

There was a horrible, sickening pain throughout my body. It almost felt as though a giant open hand in my stomach had begun to close, drawing my insides together.

Someway the idea struck my feverish mind that I ought to buy some water. I don't know where I thought I would buy it or from whom. But I began trying to figure out what I had that I could exchange for water.

At first I decided I would give my two cameras and my six-shooter for just one glass of water. Soon, however, I had added my car and clothing and books and agreed to give them for just one sip of water!

When I didn't get any water, I began thinking of what else I might have to trade. Before going to Africa, the Princess and I had sold our home in Wheaton, Illinois, in order to get money for the trip. The money not earmarked for Africa we had given to missionary work. So I didn't have any house, or I would have thrown it into the bargain. I had less than one hundred dollars in money but gladly offered that in addition to the cameras, gun, clothing, and car.

I was not only willing to give everything I had but was willing to settle for less water. Just a spoonful would have seemed so wonderful. Then it occurred to me how refreshing it would be if only I could plunge a finger into water and then put that finger in my mouth.

It was then that I remembered the cry of the rich man in Hell, *"...have mercy on me, and send Lazarus, that he may dip the tip of his finger in water, and cool my tongue; for I am tormented in this flame."*

It had never before even occurred to me that the rich man had only requested the drop or so of water that might cling to a man's finger! But it certainly made sense to me now, and I could appreciate the request.

After that it seemed to me that I could hear, over and over and over again, the rich man begging, *"Send Lazarus...let him dip the tip of his finger in water and cool my tongue...Send Lazarus...."*

Eternal Verities

I don't know how in the world I managed to keep up with the other men. But I did. When we finally came to the end of the valley and could see the palm trees high up on the rim above us, I was still at the end of the line—but I was still there!

I did drop further and further behind when we began the long climb up, up, and up. Using the tall grass as hand holds, we slowly made our way to the plateau above. All of us were exhausted and soaked with sweat when we finally reached the top.

A few minutes later we were sprawled out in the shade, sipping that wonderful life-giving water!

At first, Mr. Paul gave me about one tablespoonful in a tin cup. Then he spread a wet cloth over my face.

Several hours later, when we had finished the water and had slept, we drove to the revival service. The swelling had gone from my tongue and lips, but it was still very difficult for me to speak and the message was brief that night.

Many times, in the days that followed, I dreamed about that dreadful day. Again and again, I was awakened when I came to the place where the rich man began crying for the wet finger of Lazarus.

And hundreds of times, in my waking moments, I have contemplated the plight of the rich man in Hell.

Of course, that man could have been saved and should have been saved. But doubtless, he gave the salvation of his soul little consideration—until it was too late.

Good Neighbor, isn't it strange that all of us have a tendency to ignore eternal verities until it is too late! All of us realize we are going to die one day. We all believe the Bible that says, *"And as it is appointed unto men once to die, but after this the judgment"* (Hebrews 9:27). And yet those who are lost go on without Christ. And those of us who are saved do not get excited about our unsaved friends and loved ones until it is too late.

I'm sure all of us have considered the fact that the rich man must have bitterly regretted that he never had turned to Christ for forgiveness and salvation.

But I wonder how many of us have ever considered the fact that Lazarus, too, may have bitterly regretted that he had not won the other to Christ!

Death is real. Heaven is real. Hell is real. All of us need to face these simple truths and we need to face them now.

My unsaved friend, I urge you to turn to Jesus Christ and be saved today. Proverbs 27:1 says, *"Boast not thyself of tomorrow; for thou knowest not what a day may bring forth."*

And Hebrews 2:3 asks an obvious question, *"How shall we escape if we neglect so great salvation?"*

I urge you to take warning from the rich man who died and went to Hell when he could have been saved. And, my Christian friend, let me remind you that if you are ever going to win your loved one, if you are ever going to give out a gospel tract, preach a sermon, sing a song, or witness in any way for Christ—you must do it now, while you live, and while your unsaved friend lives.

15

TWO CHIEFS AND JIM BELL

Two Tall African Chiefs, One of Them a Cannibal, Played Vital Roles in One of the World's Greatest Mission Stations

Two men stood one day on a Congo mountain and gazed at the terrain below. One of them was a white man from America and the other a coal-black African. But the two men were brothers—brothers in Christ. Or perhaps I should say they were father and son, for the handsome, broad-shouldered Jim Bell had led Sua to Christ.

The name Sua means "Utterly Worthless," a name given him by his parents in order to fool the Devil. Surely *Satani* would not bother to harm a babe so despised of his parents! But Sua, the tall, slim, keeneyed native chief was not worthless to God, nor was he worthless to Jim Bell. They were not only brothers in Christ, they were friends and fellow-missionaries who were now setting out on a journey, from which their families and friends never expected to see them return alive.

The Deadly Jungle of Ituri

Hawks circled, floated, and dived around them in search of the various-colored rock lizards. A blazing, biting, blinding, blistering tropical sun hung overhead in the heavens. On the plains below them were herds of antelope and buffalo. Down in the river a herd of elephants splashed cooling water over their backs and squealed in delight.

But the two men on the mountain had eyes for none of those things. They were scanning the vast Ituri jungle they called the Dark Forest that began below them and stretched back some five or six hundred miles to the sea.

The Dark Forest

This is a vast, mysterious, and unmapped region comprising thousands upon thousands of square miles of the densest jungle in all Africa. Great trees growing tall and crooked are so thick that the sun cannot shine through, leaving the jungle floor always shady and dark. Hence the name, Dark Forest. Lush tropical plants, vines, and creepers make a network of vegetation that the traveler must crawl under or cut his way through with a machete. At night the darkness is so thick one can almost feel it—a veritable green Carlsbad Cavern. The rotted vegetation under foot is always damp. The air is still, hot, and steamy.

And death lurks in the mysterious jungle. Perhaps death tears out the throat with the teeth of a leopard, rips into the heart in the shape of a poisoned arrow, or enters the blood stream in some dreaded tropical disease. In one way or another, death stalks through the jungle, and that is why the tearful wives and fellow-missionaries had bid them good-bye so sadly. Hardly anyone expected ever to see these men again for they planned to explore far into the green depths of the Dark Forest.

He Called It Oicha (O-wee-chee)

As the two men stood on the mountain and looked at the awesome jungle stretched out before them, neither spoke for a long time. Finally, the white man broke the silence.

"Sua," he said, pointing to the jungle below, "in that forest there are thousands of Pygmies. They have never once heard of Jesus Christ. You and I must tell them. But, Sua, how in the world are we going to do it? How will we be able to find them? How will we make friends with them? How can we learn their language…?"

The black chief shook his head slowly.

"Only God knows, White Man," he said. Then, with simple resolution, he added, "let us go!"

With that, the two men began making their way down the side of the mountain to enter the Ituri.

They went! God bless them! They went!

It was seven months later—after their family and friends had mourned them as dead and conducted a memorial service—that the two men returned. They were haggard, gaunt, ragged, sick, and desperately weary. But they returned with joy in their hearts and wonderful news.

They had located, made friends with, and lived among the Pygmies. More than that, *Bwana* Jim Bell had selected a jungle location for work among the little people.

He called it Oicha (O-wee-chee).

Chief Kisobe

But to build a mission station, Jim Bell had to go through government channels. This meant he must get permission of the Belgian officials, then the district chief, and then the local chief. The latter was a tall, tough, wicked man named Kisobe.

This chief wanted a mission station in his neighborhood just like he wanted to grab a leopard by the tail. He wasn't the least bit interested in the white man's God. He had enough gods to worry about already. Nor was he interested in the white man's clinic—he had a rip-roaring good witch doctor that could handle anything the evil spirits could dish out.

Bwana Jim talked and argued until he was blue in the face, but he made no headway. In fact, he was making progress backwards. At first the chief simply said *te*, meaning "no." But as Jim Bell continued to talk, the *te* became *boyo te*. *Boyo* means "yes" and by saying "yes no," he meant, "Yes, I positively will not give permission!"

This went on for several hours, and Jim Bell was on the verge of giving up when he brought up a point that struck a nerve.

"Kisobe," he said, "if we had a mission station at Oicha, we would build a school. Your children could attend. Now, do you want people to think that the children of Chief Kisobe are stupid! Your children need to go to school so that all the people will say, 'The children of Chief Kisobe are very smart.'"

That did it! It was this appeal to his pride that caused Chief Kisobe to give the land for the station at Oicha.

It was a decision the chief regretted many, many times in the years to come.

The Chief Liked Pygmies

Before long, a number of people from Kisobe's village went to hear *Bwana* Jim Bell preach the Gospel of Christ. I doubt if the chief cared whether or not his friends believed in *Jesu Christo Bamaboli Munga Baba Yeato*, Jesus Christ the Son of the Heavenly Sky God. But what did bother Kisobe was the fact that, after having accepted Jesus Christ as Saviour and Lord, the natives' lives were changed. No longer would they indulge in the night-long orgies he loved so well.

What was worse—they did not believe he should continue in his horrible sins either.

Make no mistake about it, the chief was a wicked sinner. In fact, he had at least one special sin that was uncommon even among his tribe.

When Jim Bell asked Kisobe how he liked Pygmies, the chief casually answered that he liked them very much—especially the buttocks and breasts! And he liked the feet, too—they were salty!

Chief Kisobe was a cannibal!

The Revival Campaign at Oicha

Twenty-one years after Jim Bell and Sua stood together on the mountain overlooking the Ituri jungle, I stood on that same mountain. I, too, looked down at the jungle. And in my heart, I thanked God for the noble men who had gone on before. I was on my way, with the Austin Pauls and the native quartet, to Oicha to conduct a revival campaign.

Jim Bell had originally selected the site, cleared the jungle and put up a number of houses in order to reach the Pygmies. Ironically, however, there were now no Pygmies at Oicha. They do not usually stay at one place for a very long time. They are wanderers who follow game from season to season. Because of their cunning and bravery, the Pygmies are probably the most successful hunters of the jungle. Their houses are simply made with a skeleton of pliable limbs covered with large banana leaves. A large, round house can be built in an hour's time by two women. It is no problem, then, for them to leave one location and move to another.

God gave us a wonderful revival campaign. Those from the leper village were invited to attend also, and they came, literally, by the thousands. According to Austin Paul, the evening attendance averaged more than seven thousand—and this despite the fact that we were almost rained out the last service.

The meetings were held out-of-doors. A small platform was erected in front of the church and the natives sat on the ground. (In the churches, they sat on the floor. It is absolutely amazing how many can be packed into a fairly small auditorium. Men sit on one side and women on the other. A native will sit with his legs spread wide. Another sits immediately in front of him with his legs spread wide. An entire row is formed this way, with each man sitting on the floor between the legs of the fellow behind him! The rows are pressed tightly together with an occasional narrow aisle or no aisles at all.)

During most of the Oicha campaign *Bwana* Jim Bell was absent. He was at Biasiku, some miles away, where he was establishing a new mission base. It was to be headquarters for his work among the Pygmies. But he returned to Oicha for the last Saturday night's service. He was impressed with the great crowd; and his heart was stirred when he saw the large number, including a witch doctor and the wife of another witch doctor, come forward to be saved. He stayed behind to counsel with the new converts.

Later that night, he came to me (I was a guest in his home) and told me that when he retired from the field he was going to accept the pastorate of some church in Georgia. He wanted me to promise that I would come to be with him in a revival campaign. I promised and several years later, we had a wonderful revival meeting in Colquett, Georgia.

The Conversion of Kisobe

The next night was the last time I ever preached at Oicha. Because of heavy rains we could not meet out-of-doors or even in the leaky church. We met in the medical tabernacle that was not nearly large enough to hold those who wanted to come. At the last minute it stopped raining and several thousand gathered outside the roof—many more outside than inside.

Before the service, Jim Bell had said to me, "Bill, there is an old chief near here who is dying. That chief befriended me when I first came to this field. Again and again, I have tried to win him, but I have failed. I am going to go and get him in my car and bring him to this service tonight. Someway I feel it will be his last opportunity ever to be saved. And, Bill, I don't want my old friend to die without trying at least once more to win him to Christ."

Just as the service began, *Bwana* Jim's car drove up and he parked it near the platform just outside the tabernacle. In the rear seat sprawled Kisobe.

At first he seemed uninterested in the singing and preaching. But when I began to tell of the rich fool whose soul was required before he was ready, Kisobe began to listen with interest. I described the rich man—a man with many goats, many cows, many chickens, and many francs. A man so rich he lived in a house that even had more than two rooms! He was a very prosperous chief—but he was a fool because he died unsaved.

When I finished, I asked those who wished to be saved to come forward for instruction. Without a song, scores came forward.

In the back seat of Jim Bell's car, Kisobe stirred and said, "I am ready to go."

The missionary was keenly disappointed. "You mean you want to go home already?"

"No," Kisobe said, "I don't want to go home, I want to go down there where the others are going and be saved tonight." With that, the old chief pushed open the rear door of the Chevrolet and stepped to the ground. Supported between two of his young men, the old chief came forward to meet me.

When the great crowd realized it was Kisobe who was coming forward, there was almost total silence for a moment. Then a murmur spread over the vast crowd, as those near the front spread the news to those behind that Kisobe had turned to Christ. It was a time of tears and praise that many of us will never forget.

The Surrender of Sua

Several weeks later, we were in a revival campaign in Aru where God gave another wonderful revival . But the high point of those meetings came for me one day at the close of the morning services. A native, taller than I, came to me in tears. He was thin and slightly stooped and he was wearing what appeared to be an old-fashioned night-shirt over a pair of blue serge trousers.

I sent for one of the missionaries who could interpret for us and asked the old fellow what he wanted to speak to me about.

He sat with bowed head and his voice shook with emotion as he told me how he had been saved many years ago. Once he had served the Lord wholeheartedly. But now he had become backslidden and had been living in sin. He truly repented, he said, and was willing to make restitution to those he had wronged.

I read him I John 1:9, *"If we confess our sins, he is faithful and just to forgive us our sins, and to cleanse us from all unrighteousness."* I explained that God still loved him and would forgive him.

After a while, we knelt together and he poured out his heart to God in prayer, confessing his sins and rededicating his life to the Lord Jesus.

Gurney Harris, superintendent of Aru, and Austin Paul were absolutely overjoyed, and I was too, when they told me who the old man was. He was Sua, the chief who had accompanied *Bwana* Jim Bell on that historic journey into the jungle twenty-one years before!

Sua, God bless him, had come back home!

16

THE LEPERS
OF OICHA

In the Congo, Ugandi and much of the Sudan, Austin Paul was "Mr. Evangelist." With his quartet of native trumpeters, he conducted revival campaigns tirelessly from village to village. Yet, when I was there he played the role of advance man, coordinator, chief cook and bottle washer, and Pie-wagon driver. He insisted that I do most of the preaching in the great revivals and in the incidental meetings in villages and marketplaces. Although he had endured a cancer operation only two years before, he was the most energetic and tireless worker I have ever had to work with in a series of revival campaigns.

He would select a good location for a meeting place and then send messengers to all the villages within miles and miles of the place. "Come and hear a tall man who has come across the waters in a big bird," he directed the runners to say. "He has a message straight from God and you must come and hear him. Bring your wives and your children and enough food to last for seven days."

He usually led the song service, joined the brass quartet for special numbers, and he usually preached in one of the morning services. He also directed counseling of converts.

The days were long, the sun was hot, the work was hard, and I suffered a severe attack of malaria—(1 lost thirty-eight pounds before you could say *scat!*)—AND I had the time of my life.

But never, I think, did I enjoy any revival campaign more than the one at Oicha (O-wee-chee).

Dr. Carl Becker

I suppose Oicha should be thought of as a divided village. Two kinds of natives live there—those who have leprosy and their families, and those who do not have leprosy and their families. It is the home of the second largest leper colony in all the world. In the leper village there were four thousand people who had the disease, and with their wives and children they made up a population of some ten thousand.

And in Oicha there was a hospital that could take care of more than two hundred bed patients. And there was also a clinic. In fact, had there been no hospital there would have been no Oicha.

The life of the entire village—socially, physically and spiritually—revolved around a missionary doctor of medicine and surgery named Carl K. Becker.

Now, I am constantly engaged in a revival, conference and editorial ministry that keeps me in contact with hundreds of preachers and missionaries. And I like the great majority of gospel workers that I have met. But I have met few men in all my life that I learned to admire and respect and love on short acquaintance as I did Dr. Becker. His dedication to Christ made me feel worldly, his zeal made me feel like a sluggard, his modesty made me feel like a braggart, his efficiency made me feel like a stumble-bum, and his humility made me feel vain and proud by comparison.

He and Mrs. Becker graciously entertained me in their home, and he attended the evening revival services and as many of the other services as he could be spared from the hospital. When I was not in the services, I usually visited in the hospital and watched him, hour after hour, perform operations.

I think I never spent an hour with the man that I did not leave under conviction that drove me, before retiring that night, to my knees in repentance and confession.

The Pygmy With the Peg Leg

I mentioned that I watched Dr. Becker operate. One day I asked if I might bring my cameras into the operating room and take pictures. He readily agreed, but asked that I not take any pictures of his face. He did not want any publicity, he said. If there was anything worthwhile in his ministry he wanted people to think of it as typical of all missionary workers. So, one bright afternoon, I set up the movie camera on its tripod, made sure the slide camera was loaded, took light exposures, and permitted a nurse to dress me in a white coat, gauze mask, and white cap.

He operated on one patient after another. I imagine that Dr. Becker performs more major operations in one term than most surgeons do in a lifetime. I never saw anything like it.

A man suffering from a strangulated hernia was brought in. With swift, sure fingers Dr. Becker made the incision, repaired the damage, and sewed up the patient. Another man was brought in. The doctor made an imaginary line with the tip of a finger and then took a thin little knife and opened that man up like a watermelon! I broke into a sweat and piggly wigglys ran up and down my backbone like a window curtain.

The next patient was a tiny Pygmy woman. For some reason or other she had tried to run away from her newly-married husband. She didn't get very far, however, for he had picked up a bow and had shot an arrow through her leg!

After waiting several days, he had brought her to Dr. Becker. Her leg was swollen and discolored and it stank. As Dr. Becker examined the wound he remarked on the stench. (He said the leg sure was "high.")

A native nurse brought him an instrument that looked like an oversized stainless steel hacksaw. She also handed him a long shallow pan and a bottle of alcohoL He put the saw in the pan, poured alcohol over it, and set it afire. This was the quickest way to sterilize the instrument, he explained to me, when there was an emergency. And this, he assured me, was an emergency. He could not save the girl's leg, but he thought he could save her life.

A few minutes later, as I recorded it on colored film, he sawed the little woman's leg off about one inch above the knee. However, he cut the skin in such a way that a flap containing the kneecap was left intact. This he folded under so the kneecap fit over the end of the bone. As he sewed the kneecap in place, he explained that this would give her a hard stump that would fit nicely on the end of a peg leg.

Incidentally, I was not the only one who had watched the operation with fascination. The little Pygmy woman had watched, too. He had given her a spinal anesthetic and she had been fully conscious throughout the entire operation.

When Dr. Becker had made the last stitch, he bowed his head and said, "We thank thee, Lord, that we have been able to save her life. Now help us to win her to Christ."

Leprosy, a Type of Sin

Great crowds of lepers, along with the other natives, attended the revival campaign. Scores of them were saved.

Several times, during the day, I walked through the leper colony. I had never dreamed there were so many different kinds of leprosy. On some the disease had a peculiar shrinking effect. A man would hold up a hand on which he had only short stubs for fingers, but the fingernails were still in place. Others had red streaks that look something like chicken-wire fence just beneath the surface of their skin. Others had large gaping sores filled with pus. Still others had angry red holes in their hands or feet or legs where the flesh had dropped out.

Some could move around easily, while others moved as though crippled with arthritis or rheumatism. Although it is believed that this leprosy is not identical with the leprosy of the Old Testament, the two diseases do have a great deal in common.

Men had no cure for leprosy in Bible times and there was no cure for leprosy at Oicha. There were drugs that would alleviate the pain and there were drugs that would sometimes arrest the disease. But those who were lepers would die lepers.

Leprosy is a type of sin. Like leprosy, sin brings death. And, like leprosy, man has no cure for sin. Jesus Christ, through the miracle of His death and resurrection, can cleanse a sinner.

Only part of the people of Oicha were lepers. But all of us are sinners. The Bible plainly says, *"For all have sinned and come short of the glory of God"* (Romans 3:23).

It is heartbreaking that every leper cannot be healed of his leprosy. But it is an even greater tragedy that every person *will* not be saved from his sins.

Good Neighbor, God loves you and Christ died for your sins. How foolish and how tragic it will be if you reject the Saviour who alone can forgive your sins and take you to Heaven. As earnestly as I know how to say it, I urge you to turn to Jesus Christ and trust Him to save you, and I urge you to do it right now.

17

A LEOPARD SKIN FOR THE RANCH HOUSE

Our ministry has taken the Princess and me to many, many foreign lands—literally around the world. As mementos of these journeys, we have in our home and in our offices: tom-toms from the Indies, grotesque masks from the Philippines, carvings of ivory and ebony from Africa and India, tapestries from Damascus, alabaster carvings from Lebanon, innumerable objects from Palestine and Egypt, etc.

In Africa I accumulated, haphazardly and more or less accidentally, quite a collection of bows and arrows, spears, shields, knives, an exquisite "bridge" of elephants carved from a giant elephant tusk, baskets, wood carvings, and other artifacts. Some of these were given me by missionaries, some by natives, and some I purchased. I had no prepared list of items I wished to acquire, but just bought those things that appealed to me when I chanced to have an opportunity to purchase them.

Although there was no list of things I wanted to bring back from Africa, there was one thing I did want—I wanted a nice leopard skin to put on the living room wall of the house we hoped to build someday on the Bill Rice Ranch.

Bwana Paul told me that leopard skins were no longer plentiful. In the first place, chiefs liked to wear leopard skin. It is a prestige thing, a badge of distinction, a sign of royalty. And chiefs usually get first chance at available leopard skins.

In the second place, it is a rare thing if a native kills a leopard with one well-placed arrow. It is more likely the leopard will be killed by a group of hunters who hack him to bits with spears, machetes, and axes. This leaves the hide, of course, ripped and torn in dozens of places.

In the third place, the animals are often skinned carelessly. Bits of flesh and fat clinging to the hide make it impossible to properly tan the skin.

Bwana Paul said, however, that since we had several months I would doubtless have opportunities to purchase several good leopard skins for that ranch house wall.

Market Meetings

We had innumerable gospel services in the native markets. On certain days, natives from miles around gathered to buy, sell, or trade anything and everything they wanted to acquire or to get rid of. During the day, we would drive up in the Pie-wagon, set up our amplifying system, and make the announcement that this tall man came across the waters in a big bird with a message from God. If all or almost all spoke the *Bangala* trade language, only Austin Paul would interpret my message. If other dialects were present, we would have additional interpreters. These services, conducted beneath a broiling African sun, always left us wringing wet with perspiration and almost exhausted. But I do not remember our even conducting such a service without a number of conversions.

If there was time, after packing our equipment away and dealing with the new converts, *Bwana* Paul and I would walk through the throngs of people to see if anyone had a leopard skin for sale.

We never did find a leopard skin, but we did find almost everything else imaginable. In fact, we found some things you would not imagine in a million years!

For example, have you ever imagined yourself buying any half-chewed sugar cane! A man would strip a joint of cane and then chew all the way up and down like a man eating corn off the cob! He would chew and suck the juice and then offer the goody for sale! Pointing to his tooth prints, he would observe that he had not chewed very hard or deep—there was a lot of good juice left!

Always there would be sellers of goat milk. An old woman, completely naked except for a bit of cloth the size of a post card, would sit on the ground with a jug between her legs. She would holler to anyone and everyone that she has goat milk for sale. Finally, a prospective customer stops to trade. He must have his own jug, of course. Perhaps he has several pieces of manioc roots and offers a portion for five mouthfuls of milk. The old woman would take a large mouthful of milk from her jug and carefully spew it into his pitcher. She repeated this process five times as he counts it off on his fingers. All the time, he would carefully watch her Adam's apple—if she swallows one time during the process, he is going to howl that he is being cheated and insist that she give him a little more milk!

Fried ants are sometimes for sale when flying ants are in season. Large ant hills are individually owned and are often passed from father to son. These ants have wings when they are first hatched. They make one flying journey and then lose their wings and settle down to work the remainder of their lives. But when they are in the flying stage the natives set up ingenious traps and catch as many as they can. The ants are fried in deep palm fat and are a rare delicacy. For me, a little of this dish goes a long way—but I have eaten them.

Fresh meat is often for sale at the market. If hunters make a kill, they keep what they can use and sell the rest. After all, they have no refrigeration and it is either sell it or let it spoil.

Once some hunters killed a big elephant and the next market was held on the site. They figured it would be easier for the people to gather by the elephant than to try to move the elephant to the people! And, Friend, just let me tell you this—you ain't never seen nuthin' until you look at a big dead elephant—and suddenly a naked man comes crawling out of it! The only way for a man to get a choice cut of meat is to crawl inside. Of course, he doesn't want to get his shorts or loincloth bloody and greasy so he simply slips out of his clothing. Believe me, it is an astonishing sight.

Beside foodstuff one can usually find items of clothing, bows, arrows and spears, ornaments, and such trinkets as whistles made from bamboo or cane.

Nor was it unusual for us to see a man display a marriageable daughter. He would point out her good points—good teeth, strong and healthy, capable of bearing many children—for all the world like I might show a good Quarter Horse to a prospective buyer.

A Leopard Skin Not for Sale

The very last week I was in Africa, I still had no leopard skin. Oddly enough, we had never announced publicly that I was in the market for such an item. But *Bwana* Paul and other missionaries had made inquiries among the natives. In his inquiries, *Bwana* Paul had never told anyone that he wanted the skin for me.

And now we were in the very last revival campaign. There would be no more meetings in the marketplaces, no more services in the villages, and no more opportunities for me to try to find the one thing I had really wanted to take back home from Africa.

The week was almost gone when *Bwana* Paul excitedly told me I was going to get that leopard skin after all. There were two men attending this campaign, who had such skins. One of the hides, he understood, was really a beauty!

The next day, following the morning services, the two men met us at the Pie-wagon with their rolled-up skins. *Bwana* Paul unrolled the first one and looked at it. It was not a good hide. The pelt was not in good condition and it had been poorly cared for. Nevertheless, *Bwana* Paul asked, "*Óya ozi franco boni* (How many francs do you want?)" The price the native wanted was so high that Mr. Paul's hair-trigger temper went off with a bang! The price was outrageous, he declared. Too much even for an excellent skin.

He then unrolled the other fellow's merchandise, and we both gasped in appreciation. It was, I think, the most beautiful leopard skin I have ever seen. It was beautifully colored and had been carefully tanned.

Bwana Paul asked, "*Óya ozi franco boni.*" The man shook his head, smiled, and replied, "This is not for selling."

I looked at the fellow. He looked familiar. He was a large, well-built man, with a handsome, intelligent looking face. He was dressed in a pair of faded khaki shorts. I knew I had seen him before, but just supposed it had been in the current revival campaign.

Bwana Paul was both puzzled and in a bad humor. Of course the fellow wanted to sell it. What would he do with it? It was an excellent skin and he would pay a little more than for an average skin.

Still smiling and shaking his head, the man would only repeat, "It is not for selling."

Finally, exasperated, *Bwana* Paul asked, "Well, if it is not for selling, what is it for?"

"It is for giving," he replied very simply.

He quietly took the hide back from *Bwana* Paul and slowly rolled it up again.

"It is for giving," he continued, "to *Bwana Machelli* (Rice) because he is my father. In his sickness, he explained to me about Jesus. By me in the dirt, he kneeled with his arm on my shoulder and prayed *Munga Baba Yeato* to forget my sins. The skin is for giving to him. In his hut he will hang it and will remember to tell his wife and his children of his people over here."

I still thought the man was one I had met in the revival we were then conducting, and I could not remember winning him to Christ. But after Mr. Paul questioned him about it for a few minutes, I did remember. The big fellow had been saved in another revival campaign weeks ago and many miles away.

He had come to me at noontime following the third service of the morning. A native pastor had preached first, then Austin Paul, and then I had spoken and given an invitation. As usual, I was soaking wet with perspiration due to vigorous preaching, the hot sun, and malaria. As a rule, I stayed while the missionaries dealt with the new converts. This often took as much as two hours and sometimes longer. (The missionaries I worked with in Africa put many American pastors to shame in the careful way they dealt with and followed up new converts.) Although I could not speak their language and could not deal with them myself, I could walk around, shake hands with them, and sometimes give scriptural help through an interpreter.

The missionaries were dealing with the new converts in small groups, and I walked over to one side and sat down, I think, on the ground. It was then that Gurney Harris walked over with a large native and told me the man was in trouble and wished to talk with me. He said I looked tired and sick and wondered if I felt like talking with the man at that time. I thought I would feel fine as soon as I had a drink of water and Gurney handed me a canteen. I took a drink—and promptly threw up! (Nothing unusual—by this time I just may have been holding the world's record for regurgitation!) I motioned the two men to sit down by me and the native began to talk. The poor fellow thought himself to be the chief of all sinners. With downcast face and shame in his voice, he told me of his sins. When he had finished, I explained to him, from the Bible, the plan of salvation; told him of Jesus and His love and death for us. The conversation must have lasted well over one hour with me taking time out, once more, to vomit!

Before we parted we knelt together. I put my arm across his shoulders and prayed with him.

It was just one of the many, many such experiences, and I had forgotten it until he gave me the leopard skin. And then he reminded me of something else, too. Since that time, he had been with us in a number of revivals, having walked the long distances from one place to the other! And it had been he who had stayed so close by my side that night on the great rocks when the pride of hungry lions had moved about below. He had been determined, he said, that a lion must eat him first before it harmed me!

Tears flowed down the big fellow's face as he talked, and my own heart was stirred to its depths. When he finished, I placed the leopard skin on the front seat of the Pie-wagon and hugged him, my tears splashing on his brown shoulders.

I have forgotten his name. It was an odd one. I wrote it down but I cannot find it. But, today that beautiful leopard skin hangs in our living room on the wall, and every time I see it I am reminded of those wonderful days of soul winning and revival in Darkest Africa.

The "Rejoicing" of Soul Winning

How many good things in life have come our way because of someone we have led to Christ!

One of our first series of revival campaigns was in Oklahoma. We had already enrolled in Moody Bible Institute, but it was just before the opening of school.

In one of the churches, a former pastor had left owing money in the little town; and Cathy and I had taken our love offering to pay his debts—a suit of clothes, grocery bill, gasoline bill, etc. We had less than $10 left and our next engagement was several hundred miles away. By doing without food and sleeping in the car, we thought we could make the trip. But as we drove along that Monday evening, Betty, our baby, became quite ill. At dark we stopped in a little Western town to find a doctor. We had never been there before in all our lives. The doctor examined our baby and wrote out a prescription. His bill, he told me, was added to the cost of the prescription and I could pay the druggist for both. But when we went to the drug store and had the prescription filled, we found that the doctor had written on the bottom of the prescription, "Charge this to mine account." We rushed back to his office to thank him and he said he had recognized our names although he had never met us before. But we had met his run-away granddaughter, had won her to Christ, and had sent her back home.

That very same night we drove into a service station and ordered only two gallons of gas, believing we might find the gasoline cheaper further down the road. The filling station owner, however, filled the tank to the brim! I didn't know what to do because it would take all the money I had left to pay for that gasoline, and it would not be enough to take us where we were going. When I tried to explain the fellow smiled, showed me a handbill with my picture on it, and told me how his brother had been saved several months before in an entirely different place! The gasoline was a gift and so was a $5 bill he pressed into my hand!

At the very beginning of our ministry, then, the Princess and I realized it really was true that *"... he that winneth souls is wise"* and that God *"... is a rewarder of them that diligently seek him."*

The two incidents I mentioned are admittedly little things—but they were mighty important to us at the time. But if they are small things, try this one on for size—

Because of a sermon I had preached on adultery, a man whose daughter was a harlot threatened to kill me. He was wicked and mean and had shot two men. One night, while I was preaching, he and the daughter stormed in the back door of the church, came down the aisle, and confronted me. Pulling a Colt .38 he yelled, "Bill Rice, I am going to blow you to Hell!" There was no way in the world I could reach him before he pulled that trigger! Women screamed and fainted and men ran or ducked for cover. As I looked down the barrel of that gun, I thought I was looking at certain death. I was so sure of it that I made my farewell address! "Tell Cathy I love her and tell John Rice to preach my funeral. Now—you go ahead and pull that trigger!"

It sounds brave but actually it was hopeless defiance. I had given myself up as dead, when two men I had won to Christ sprang into action. One grabbed the gun, the other jumped in front of me to protect my body with his own!

I could write a book on the blessings that have come my way in life because of someone I have won to Jesus Christ. The Bill Rice Ranch is headquarters of the largest missionary work to the Deaf in all the history of all the world. I often receive letters from preachers asking how we raise the multiplied thousands of dollars each year to maintain this ministry. People know that I am an independent Baptist evangelist—that I do not belong to any organization of churches, do not belong to any convention, am not underwritten by any secular or religious organization in all the world. So, many write every year to ask how we have raised the hundreds of thousands of dollars it has taken to maintain this work.

I am afraid that many are disappointed when I reply simply and truthfully, that almost all of the money comes in through people we have won—directly or indirectly—to Christ!

Thousands of people from around the world have seen that leopard skin on our living room wall and have heard the story of the man who gave it to me.

My own heart has been warmed—from top to bottom—again and again as it has reminded me of those wonderful months I spent in Darkest Africa with some of God's most devoted servants, winning the lost to Christ. At that time—and hundreds of times since, I have found Psalm 126:6 to be true, *"He that goeth forth and weepeth, bearing precious seed, shall doubtless come again with rejoicing, bringing his sheaves with him."*

The Austin Pauls—Missionaries

The Sid Langfords—Missionaries

The Harold Amstutzes—Missionaries

Native Preacher, Austin Paul, and Blind Paula

Missionary Bennett Williams at Semliki Camp

With the King's Commandant—One of the Bravest Men
I Have Ever Known

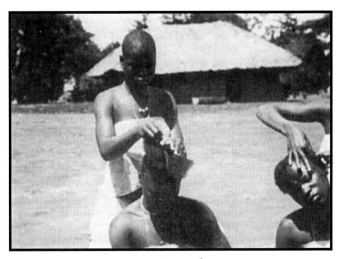

Beauty Parlor

Re-packing the Pie-wagon After Village Service

Graduates of Moody Bible Institute in Africa

A Morning Revival Crowd

Solomono

Ephrenoto

Methuselah

Juano

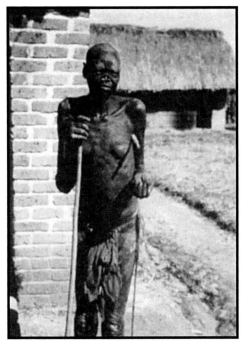

The Leper of Oicha

Jim Bell at Oicha—Missionary to Lepers

Lotuka Spearmen—They Charged

Bill Rice With Gabani, His Wife, and Baby—He Was the Second Pygmy Convert

Funeral of Elderly Christian Woman

Author With Harold Amstutz and Trackers

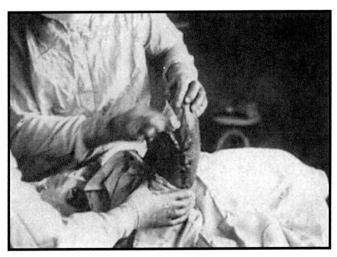

Preparing Pygmy for Peg Leg

Carrying Sick Girl in Sling

The Austin Pauls, Solomono, and Methuselah

African Dancer

Hunting Wild Elephants

Elephants' Evening Bath and Drink in the River

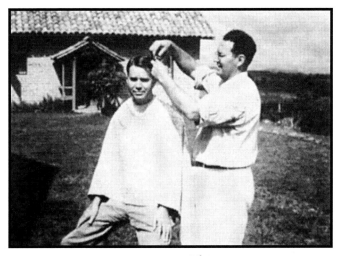

Haircut in Africa

A Leopard Skin for the Ranch House

Chief and Son (Backs to Camera)
Wearing Leopard Skins

Scorpion

Half-Grown Buffalo

Up Periscope!

"Timbu, Bwana, Timbu!
(Elephant, White Boss Man, Elephant)"

Simba, the Africa Lion

"Baboon"—Dangerous Thief and Enemy

Good-by—please pray for us
as the Lord lays it on your heart.
Bill Rice